⚜ Rosie Wells Enterprises, Inc. ⚜

Secondary Market Price Guide for Precious Moments® Company Dolls

This tag is an example of a doll tag having the likeness of a specific doll. This tag was the first tag to have Sam's name on it.

Editor and Publisher: Rosie Wells
Contributing Co-Editor: Jan Kropenick
22341 E. Wells Rd., Canton, IL 61520

Phone: 1-309-668-2211   Fax: 1-309-668-2795

Visit our Web Site! http://www.RosieWells.com

E-Mail address: RosieWells@aol.com

©1997 Precious Moments, Inc. Licensee, Rosie Wells Enterprises, Inc.
"Precious Moments®" is a registered trademark of Precious Moments, Inc. All Rights Reserved.

From the Editor

Imagine a world without dolls. It is very hard to do! Cloth dolls, beautiful "porcelain look" faced dolls with elaborate fabric and intricate lace gowns, baby dolls of every size, dolls of every nationality; the Precious Moments Company Dolls have come to be that and much more. It is with great pleasure that Rosie Wells Enterprises, Inc., presents this guide to you… the collector of these beautiful dolls.

Those who began collecting these dolls in 1985, with the Jonathan & David doll line, the original licensor of Precious Moments artwork, have seen this line grow and change with the name changes of the company. When Jonathan & David closed its doors only a few years after introducing the vinyl doll line, it was continued by Precious Moments Country of Carthage, Missouri - a company owned by family members of Sam Butcher. Eventually, Precious Moments Country became Precious Moments Company, and continues to operate its business from Carthage, Missouri. The dolls, which were intended for children - to be played with and loved, caught the attention of some observant Precious Moments collectors, who kept those original nine dolls clean and neat, on display. Fourteen years later, the popularity of these vinyl dolls has grown to what it is today.

For the past 15 years, Precious Moments collectibles have been a big influence in my life. The stir of Precious Moments collecting was what started me publishing my own magazine for Precious Moments collectors. Like so many mothers, buying a Precious Moments doll for my little girl is but a memory. Now, I look forward to buying Precious Moments dolls for a granddaughter, due this fall. As I watch her grow, I will see her collection of Precious Moments dolls grow, just as countless mothers, grandmothers and Precious Moments doll collectors have done in the past.

We are very happy to have the top authority on Precious Moments Company Dolls as co-editor and research analyst for this guide. Jan Kropenick and I have known each other for many years, and we share the same enthusiasm for Precious Moments collecting. Jan has been more involved with the Precious Moments Company Dolls than I have, and definitely was the person to supply the collector information for this guide. Many of the "rare" doll photos are Jan's dolls.
This guide has been written for you, the collector, with information which we feel is important for you to keep in mind while collecting and enjoying your Precious Moments Company Dolls.

Your input, collection photos and questions are welcomed. You are a special reason Precious Moments Company Dolls are so popular! Enjoy them! Share with others this guide and collecting information. The more who collect with you, the more popular the dolls become. Thus the thrill of a collectible continues to grow in the hearts of new collectors every day!

Rosie

Dedication

I would like to dedicate this guide to the late Phil Butcher, son of Sam Butcher. Phil was a very special person who put a ray of sunshine into the lives of everyone who met him. If you didn't have a smile, he gave you one. When life's storm clouds were overhead, he would make sure that his contagious laughter spilled over into your life to put a rainbow in the sky. Of course, his glasses slipped down to the end of his nose while he was laughing, but he would just push them up again without it bothering his happiness.

He was a "Big Brother" to the folks at Precious Moments Company, and all felt they were a part of his family.

God did not take Phil from us, but He did carry him home. I am reminded of an old favorite hymn in which the lyrics sing, "When they ring those golden bells for you and me." I like to think of Phil laughing as he is trying to have the loudest bell in heaven to welcome his loved ones home.

Phil was also a great dad, as he loved spending quality time with his children. They loved it when the he took them skeet shooting, and he would throw objects in the air as a target to aim at. I'm sure that the object in the air was seldom hit, but Phil's aim to let his children know how much he loved them was in the range of hitting the center of the bull's eye of the target of his love.

In I Corinthians 13:13, "And now abideth faith, hope, charity, these three; but the greatest of these is charity." Thanks to Phil, his charity was in the form of laughter which brought much of God's sunshine into our lives.

Jan

Acknowledgements

I wish to thank Rosie Wells for the privilege of co-editing this PMC doll guide. My heavenly Father always gives me the courage and direction in composing an article, and He has always answered my prayers when the mountain seemed too high to climb. Many thanks to Craig Schoenhals, CEO of Precious Moments Co., Inc., and Kristi Hodkin of PMC Telemarketing for answering my numerous calls searching for accurate information. Needless to say, they are such loving, caring and sharing people who love their work. It is wonderful to have a dear friend, Joann Chuirazzi, who was willing to send dolls to be photographed, and who supplied me with accurate information for all the exclusive dolls. Many thanks to the staff at Rosie Wells Enterprises, Inc. Rosie must know God loves her as she is blessed with such a wonderful staff!

Jan Kropenick

Jan Kropenick is very well known among Precious Moments Company Doll collectors. Jan resides in Florida with her husband, John. They are parents of five children and grandparents to three grandsons and one granddaughter. Jan says, "We are all children of God, no matter what our age may be, and there is a child within each and every person. No one is ever too old to receive a teddy bear or a doll, which lets us all know love goes on forever."

Research and secondary market prices were provided by Jan Kropenick.

Table of Contents

From the Editor II
From Jan Kropenick III
Table of Contents. IV
History of the Dolls V
Doll Index by Name i
Plush Index by Name iv
How To Use This Guide VI
Jonathan & David Dolls 1
Chapel Exclusive 4
Precious Moments Company Exclusive Doll 10
General Line 11
Twenty-six Inch General Line Dolls 34
Preferred Doll Retailers 35

Doll Collections and Series

Berry Best Friends 40	Mommy, I Love You Series 74
Birthday Wishes 41	Native American Dolls 1 76
Career Series 41	Native American Dolls 2 78
Children of the World 42	Nativity .80
Christmas Classic Doll Collection .52	Nursery Rhymes Series 80
Christmas Tree Toppers, Ornaments and Decorations 53	Pearls & Lace Series 81
Classic Doll Collection 57	Plaid Rag Dolls 81
Four Seasons Doll Collection 59	Precious Jewel Doll Series 83
Garden of Friends 1 61	Precious Pals 89
Garden of Friends 2 65	Songs of the Spirit 90
Garden of Friends 3 68	Sweetheart Series 91
Military Series 72	Wooden Doll Series 93

Special Edition

Amway Dolls 94
House of Lloyd 96
Karate Dolls 97
LTD Exclusive 97
Publishers' Clearing House 99
QVC 100
Spiegel Exclusive 103
Sports Doll Collection from Hy-Vee 103

Hi Babies, A Sam Butcher Original 105
Plush 113
History of Tags 122
Suspended, Retired List, Limited Edition,
Sold Out and Discontinued 125
Subject Index 128
Notes

By
Jan Kropenick

The History of Precious Moments® Dolls

In the beginning, God created man. Then, in our life time, God created a very special man named Samuel J. Butcher.

As a little boy he wanted to spend most of his time drawing, but his dad insisted that he needed to go outside and play with his brothers and sister. Being a very obedient son, Sam went outside to play. Tucking his boyish sadness into a portion of his little heart, it would later be used as his trademark of "teardrop eyes."

Monetarily, his family counted pennies, but he was blessed with a family filled with love. Beginning with his Grandma Martha to the youngest of his grandchildren, Sam Butcher knows that "Love covers all."

As a young man, he met Rev. Royal Blue, "who loves to tell the Story" and encouraged Sam to walk with the Lord. Since that time, Sam's heart has been filled with joy, knowing, "He leadeth me." He has been led up to the mountains and down into the valleys and he has had days without sunshine, but he knows God will never leave him nor forsake him.

Sam began his ministry in child evangelism with his "Chalk Talks" and illustrations on Christian record covers and books.

He and his partner, Bill Beil, converted an old building into the Jonathan & David Company. One of Sam's first greeting cards exemplifies his hopes and dreams of spreading God's love to all nations.

In 1981, Sam and Bill were led to the Philippines, where they had their dolls made and where they expanded their Christian ministry. They gave financial assistance to young Bible School students. What better way to send a message via two Precious Moments dolls than producing the Jesus Loves Me boy and girl!

The Jonathan & David Company moved to a larger facility. It was easily identified by the two angels on a cloud, Love Goes On Forever, over the front door.

In 1986, five-inch dolls were made exclusively for the Samuel J. Butcher Company and distributed in the United States by the Samson Company (Sam's sons, Jon and Philip). Due to Sam's semi-retirement of approximately one year, Jon had to direct his entire time toward being spokesman for the Samuel J. Butcher Company. He did a fantastic amount of work preparing for Sam's return to the States. Later, everyone realized "semi-retirement from public appearances" meant that Sam would walk and talk with the Lord to put his ideas and dreams into reality.

In 1987, the Precious Moments Chapel complex began to develop into a reality, and the Samson Company quietly closed their doors in order to focus on the Chapel.

The Jonathan & David Company had produced nine Precious Moments dolls over a span of three years, but, in 1988, their doors would also close. When one door closes, God will always open another.

Precious Moments Country, Incorporated, opened their doors in 1989 and continued to distribute the Jesus Loves Me boy and girl dolls, Taffy and Toto clown dolls, Sailor Sam and Private JoJo. They continued the production of Blue Missy for one year, Patti with Goose for two years, and revised Pink Missy and produced her until 1995.

In 1992, Precious Moments Country, Inc., was changed to Precious Moments Company, Inc., and the door remained open to continued expansion of the doll industry as we know it today.

Dolls Index By Name

- [ ] 4th of July 7" and 9" 9

A

- [ ] African-American Baby 29
- [ ] African-American Baby 24
- [ ] Air Force Boy 73
- [ ] Air Force Girl 73
- [ ] Aisha - Africa 50
- [ ] Allison - USA 51
- [ ] Alohaloni - Hawaii 51
- [ ] Amber Precious Jewel 86
- [ ] Amber Sweetheart 91
- [ ] Amy 35
- [ ] Andreah 58
- [ ] Angela 30
- [ ] Angelica 56
- [ ] Angelina - Italy 48
- [ ] April's Child 41
- [ ] Army Boy 72
- [ ] Army Girl 72
- [ ] Ashley - Fall 60
- [ ] August's Child 41

B

- [ ] Becca 98
- [ ] Benson - Basketball 103
- [ ] Beryl 85
- [ ] Bess w/map 6
- [ ] Bethany 18
- [ ] Blossom - August 63
- [ ] Blossom - August 67
- [ ] Blue and Yellow Plaid Rag Doll .. 82
- [ ] Blue Bell - February 69
- [ ] Blue Missy J & D 3
- [ ] Blue Missy PMC 12
- [ ] Blueberry 40
- [ ] Boy Clown 17
- [ ] Boy in Fatigues 74
- [ ] Boysenberry 40
- [ ] Brianna 95
- [ ] Bride Blonde 12" 29
- [ ] Bride Brunette 12" 31
- [ ] Bridget 58
- [ ] Brooke - Spring 59
- [ ] Brown Baby 24

C

- [ ] Candie 99
- [ ] Cara 36
- [ ] Carissa and Baby Tess 76
- [ ] Carla - America 42
- [ ] Carrie Ornament 54
- [ ] Carrie 54
- [ ] Casey 18
- [ ] Casey - Blond 9
- [ ] Cassie - Cheerleader 103
- [ ] Caucasian Baby 28
- [ ] Celeste 56
- [ ] Chapel Fan Doll - White 4
- [ ] Chapel Fan Doll - Black 5
- [ ] Chapel Indian Doll 5
- [ ] Charity - French Horn 90
- [ ] Chippewa 78
- [ ] Chloe 92
- [ ] Chrissy - November 64
- [ ] Chrissy - November 68
- [ ] Christie 54
- [ ] Christina 30
- [ ] Christine 98
- [ ] Christmas Hi Baby in Sleigh .. 111
- [ ] Christy 53
- [ ] Cindy 99
- [ ] Clifford 30
- [ ] Coleenia 4
- [ ] Colette 7
- [ ] Colin 19
- [ ] Colleen 26
- [ ] Cory - Phillippines 43
- [ ] Courtney 92
- [ ] Crystal 87

D

- [ ] Daisy - April 62
- [ ] Daisy - April 66
- [ ] Daisy - May 69
- [ ] Daniel 5
- [ ] Dawn and Rag Doll 23
- [ ] December's Child 41
- [ ] Delaney 21
- [ ] Desert Rose 83
- [ ] Dustin 16" 7
- [ ] Dustin 12" 8
- [ ] Dusty 21

E

- [ ] Ellie 26
- [ ] Emily 91
- [ ] Emma 57
- [ ] Erich 57
- [ ] Evie 25

F

- [ ] Faith - Harp 90
- [ ] February's Child 41
- [ ] Flint - Football 103
- [ ] Fredrick 93
- [ ] Freya - Denmark 49

G

- [ ] Gertrude 93

Dolls Index By Name

- Girl Clown 16
- Girl in Fatigues 73
- Gloria 53
- Gloria - Speigel Exclusive 103
- Gold Angel 55
- Gordon - Golf 103
- Grace 31
- Gracie 27
- Graduate 32
- Gramma's Sweetie 27
- Grandma Martha 26
- Grandpa Bill 29
- Green and Pink Plaid Rag Doll . .81
- Gretchen - Germany 47
- Gretel - Sweden 45
- Groom Blond 12" 29
- Groom Brunette 12" 31
- Guardian Angel 29

H

- Hanford - Hockey 103
- Hannah 92
- Hans (Ollie) - Austria 48
- Happy 59
- Harmony 55
- Heather 33
- Hispanic Baby 28
- Holly - December 65
- Holly - December 68
- Holly - December 71
- Hope - Trumpet 90
- Hopi Maiden 76

I

- Ian 32
- Iris - May 62
- Iris - May 66
- Iroquois 77
- Ivan - Russia 46

J

- Jacarila Apache 79
- Jackie Ann 21
- Jade 84
- Jamie 8
- Janelle 102
- Janet and Baby Sarah 74
- Janna 52
- January's Child 41
- Jasmine - January 61
- Jasmine - January 65
- Jasmine - January 68
- Jasper 88
- Jenny 15
- Jeremy 33
- Jessi Bride -16" 11
- Jessi and Baby Lisa 74
- Jessica 94

- Jessi Bride - 26" 34
- Jesus Loves Me - Girl 1
- Jesus Loves Me - Boy 1
- Jonny Brown Tuxedo 14
- Jonny Dark Grey Tuxedo 14
- Jonny Black Tuxedo 14
- Jonny Groom - 26" 34
- Jordan 15
- Josh 33
- Joy 55
- July's Child 41
- June's Child 41

K

- Karate Boy 97
- Karate Girl 97
- Kari - Holland 45
- Katherine 95
- Kathy and Donnie 75
- Katie 19
- Katlyn 36
- Keiki - Lani - Hawaii 51
- Kerri 19
- Kiesha 96

L

- Lacey 37
- Laurie & Liza 102
- Lily - March 61
- Lily - April 69
- Lily - March 66
- Lindsay 16" 7
- Lindsay 12" 8
- Lindsay 101
- Little Mary 98
- Little Missy 98
- Little Mistletoe 25
- Little Sunshine 36
- Lori and Ginnie 75
- Louise 93
- Love - Violin 90

M

- Maddy 94
- Maggie 38
- March's Child 41
- Marcy 52
- Margaret 27
- Maria - Spain 44
- Marigold - November 71
- Marissa 95
- Maureen 6
- May's Child 41
- Mazie - America 42
- Megan - Summer 60
- Mei-Mei - China 50
- Melinda 58
- Melissa 94
- Miakoda 59

vii

Dolls Index By Name

- ☐ Milly and Her New Baby Doll 22
- ☐ Misu - Japan 44
- ☐ Morning Glory - American Indian 49
- ☐ Morning Glory - March 69
- ☐ Morning Star 18

N

- ☐ Natalie 32
- ☐ Natasha .93
- ☐ Nativity Set 80
- ☐ Navajo 79
- ☐ Navy Boy 73
- ☐ Navy Girl 72
- ☐ Nicholas - PMC 23
- ☐ Nicholas - QVC 100
- ☐ Nicole .100
- ☐ Nikki 101
- ☐ Nina 10
- ☐ Noel 101
- ☐ November's Child 41

O

- ☐ October's Child 41
- ☐ Ollie - Norway 49
- ☐ Opal 87
- ☐ Ozark Andy 15" 13
- ☐ Ozark Andy 26" 34
- ☐ Ozark Annie 15" 13
- ☐ Ozark Annie 26" 34

P

- ☐ Pansy - July 63
- ☐ Pansy - July 67
- ☐ Pansy - July 70
- ☐ Pat 28
- ☐ Patti with Goose PMC 11
- ☐ Patti with Goose J&D 3
- ☐ Peace 55
- ☐ Pearl 84
- ☐ Peony - August 70
- ☐ Phillip 20
- ☐ Pink Missy 11
- ☐ Pink Missy 12
- ☐ Pink Missy 2nd Edition 12
- ☐ Pink Missy J&D 3
- ☐ Piper 28
- ☐ PM Collector Doll 6
- ☐ Princess Melody 57
- ☐ Princess Sincere 17
- ☐ Private Jo Jo 1
- ☐ Pualani - Hawaii 49
- ☐ Pumpkin - October 64
- ☐ Pumpkin - October 67
- ☐ Pumpkin - October 71

R

- ☐ Rachel .91
- ☐ Raspberry 40
- ☐ Rebecca 95
- ☐ Red and Blue Plaid Rag Doll 81
- ☐ Red Riding Hood 80
- ☐ Regina .32
- ☐ Robin 37
- ☐ Rose - June 62
- ☐ Rose - June 66
- ☐ Rose - June 70
- ☐ Rosemary 92
- ☐ Royal Blue Plaid Rag Doll 82
- ☐ Ruby 85

S

- ☐ Sadie - Softball 103
- ☐ Sailor Sam 2
- ☐ Sandy - Blue 20
- ☐ Sandy - White 20
- ☐ Sapphire 86
- ☐ Sara and Kara 37
- ☐ Sarah 25
- ☐ Seminole 78
- ☐ September's Child 41
- ☐ Shannon - Ireland 43
- ☐ Shonnie - American Indian 43
- ☐ Shoshoni 79
- ☐ Silver Angel 56
- ☐ Sioux 77
- ☐ Snuggles 96
- ☐ Sophie - Poland 48
- ☐ Star 53
- ☐ Stephanie 52
- ☐ Strawberry 40
- ☐ Sulu - Alaska Brown Suit 46
- ☐ Sulu - Alaska White Suit 46
- ☐ Sunny - September 64
- ☐ Sunny - September 67
- ☐ Sunny - September 70
- ☐ Sunshine 38
- ☐ Susan with Twins 75
- ☐ Sydney - Soccer 103

T

- ☐ Taffy 2
- ☐ Taya - India 47
- ☐ Teacher 41
- ☐ Tiffany .16
- ☐ Timmy .54
- ☐ Timmy the Angel white gown . .16
- ☐ Timmy the Angel blue w/blanket 17
- ☐ Tina - Tennis 103
- ☐ Tonya .97
- ☐ Toto 2
- ☐ Tracey .22

V

- ☐ Valerie .39
- ☐ Victoria 81
- ☐ Viola 23
- ☐ Violet - February 61
- ☐ Violet - February 65

Dolls Index By Name

W
- ☐ Welcome Home Baby - Blue ..112
- ☐ Welcome Home Baby - Yellow .112
- ☐ Welcome Home Baby - Pink ..112
- ☐ White Baby 24
- ☐ Whitney - Winter 60
- ☐ Winnie 30

Y
- ☐ Yakima 77
- ☐ Yoim - Korea 50
- ☐ Young Hee 31
- ☐ Young Ho 31

Z
- ☐ Zuni 76

Plush Index By Name

B
- ☐ Bailey Bunny 119
- ☐ Baxter 120
- ☐ Blue Bear 9" 117
- ☐ Blue Teddy Bear 12" 114
- ☐ Blue Bunny - Get Well Soon ..111
- ☐ Blue Bunny - Hoppy Birthday ..111
- ☐ Blue Bunny - I Love You 110
- ☐ Blue Bunny - Some Bunny Loves You 110
- ☐ Bride Bear 117
- ☐ Brown Teddy Bear 12" 114
- ☐ Brown Bear 9" 117

C
- ☐ Charlie Bear - 15" 115
- ☐ Charlie Bear - 21" 116
- ☐ Charlie Bear - 48" 116
- ☐ Chris Bear in Stocking 121
- ☐ Colton Corduroy 121
- ☐ Cupid Bear 118
- ☐ Dillon Denim 121
- ☐ Dudley - Dog 89

E
- ☐ Edmond 119
- ☐ Eyvette 120

G
- ☐ Georgina - Giraffe 89
- ☐ Gill - Fish 89

- ☐ Grant Bear in Stocking 120
- ☐ Grey Bear 6" 114
- ☐ Groom Bear 118

H
- ☐ Hi Bunny 111
- ☐ Hopper - Bird 89

J
- ☐ Jeremy - Tucan 89

L
- ☐ Landon 119
- ☐ Letty 119

M
- ☐ Mint Green Bunny - Some Bunny Loves You 110

P
- ☐ Parker Plaid 121
- ☐ Peach Bunny - Get Well Soon .111
- ☐ Peach Bunny - Hoppy Birthday 111
- ☐ Peach Bunny - I Love You 110
- ☐ Peach Bunny - Some Bunny Loves You 110
- ☐ Pink Bear 9" 117
- ☐ Pink Teddy Bear 12" 114
- ☐ Pink Bunny - Get Well Soon . . .111
- ☐ Pink Bunny - Hoppy Birthday ..111
- ☐ Pink Bunny - I Love You 110
- ☐ Pink Bunny - Some Bunny Loves You 110

S
- ☐ Simon - Blue Lamb 89
- ☐ Simon the lamb - Blue 115
- ☐ Simon the lamb - White 115
- ☐ Snowball 116
- ☐ Snowball w/Vest 118
- ☐ Snowflake - Rabbit 89

T
- ☐ Trevor 120

W
- ☐ White Bear 113
- ☐ White Bunny - Get Well Soon .111
- ☐ White Bunny - Hoppy Birthday 111
- ☐ White Bunny - I Love You 110
- ☐ White Bunny - Some Bunny Loves You 110

Y
- ☐ Yellow Bunny - Some Bunny Loves You 110

How To Use This Guide

①1035 ②**Philip**   ③ ☐
         ④ *Retired – December, 1994*
⑤*Comments:* Issued October, 1992, 16" Tall.
Debbie (Butcher) Cho did an exquisite portrayal of her brother, who was loved by everyone. He is dressed in a "patched" calico shirt and jeans, with a slingshot hanging out of his back pocket, denim sneakers and two angel wings that took him home to be with the Lord. Philip's tortoise shell glasses were always sliding down his nose, because he continually laughed. The first shipment of 2,000 dolls arrived with Philip wearing sunglasses, but further shipments had clear glasses.
Secondary Market Value Sunglasses: $200-250
Secondary Market Value Clear glasses: $120-150
⑥ Purchased From _____ Date_____
⑦ Orig. S.R. $50.00   I paid $_____

1   Style number

2   Doll's name

3   Instant Alert - This tells you immediately if you have this doll or not. Place a ✓ in the box if you own the doll.

4   If the doll is suspended, retired, or limited in production you will find it here in bold letters.

5   Comments: This contains the year of introduction, the height of the doll and any other pertinent information about each doll. Each year's guide may contain added information reporting; variations, changed and new information from collectors, etc.

6   The secondary market values are affected by the variations in the doll and the number of dolls produced. Use these prices as a "guide" to resell, buy or insure your collection. Always do your own research, as prices may fluctuate from time to time!

7   The "Original Suggested Retail" is shown with each entry to inform you of what price the doll debuted. You may use this line to write where you purchased the doll, the date and the price you paid and any extra detail needed for future reference.

Every effort has been made to assure this guide is complete and accurate. Use the prices in this guide only as a guide to help determine the value of your pieces for insurance evaluation.

Jonathan & David Dolls

D001   **Jesus Loves Me - girl**
                 Retired – 1988
Comments: Issued late 1984, 14" Tall.
In 1985, trim was added to the sleeves and hem of her gown. The dainty pink flower accent was taken from the upper part of her gown and placed at her neckline.
Secondary Market Value: $200-245
Purchased From _____ Date _____
Orig. S.R. $19.95   I paid $_____

D002   **Jesus Loves Me - boy**
                 Retired – 1988
Comments: Issued late 1984, 14" Tall.
His white pajamas remained unchanged throughout his production. He was known to have brown eyes but a few arrived with blue eyes. The dolls with blue eyes are considered extremely rare.
Secondary Market Value Blue Eyes: $300-325
Secondary Market Value Brown Eyes: $195-225
Purchased From _____ Date _____
Orig. S.R. $19.95   I paid $_____

D003   **Private Jo Jo**
                 "I'm In The Lord's Army"
                 Retired – 1988
Comments: Issued 1985, 14-16" Tall.
He wears a fatigue uniform, boots and a helmet. He has tan curly hair and his height varies from 14-16". He is accompanied by a numbered certificate. If he is found in his original white box with certificate, add $20.
Secondary Market Value: $250-225
Purchased From _____ Date _____
Orig. S.R. $25.00   I paid $_____

Jonathan and David

**D004   Sailor Sam
          "The Lord Is My Captain"
          *Retired – 1988***
Comments: Issued 1985, 14½-17" Tall.
Sailor Sam has either blonde or tan hair. In the 1985-1986 Jonathan & David gift catalog, he is pictured with dark brown hair, but one must assume this doll was a prototype. Sailor Sam is known to vary in height from 14½-17". If he is in his original white box with certificate, add $20.
Secondary Market Value: $200-225
Purchased From _____ Date _____
Orig. S.R. $20.00   I paid $_____

**D005   Toto
          *Retired – 1988***
Comments: Issued 1985, 14½-16" Tall.
Toto is easily identified by his purple curly hair and his cone shape molded hat. He may be found with purple, pink or white pom pons on his pastel multi-colored striped suit. His clown suit may be trimmed with white lace, gold rick-rack or yellow floral cord trim. A few clowns have been found to have silver rick-rack trim. He is wearing purple shoes. Very popular!
Secondary Market Value: $300-325
Purchased From _____ Date _____
Orig. S.R. $25.00   I paid $_____

**D006   Taffy
          *Retired – 1988***
Comments: Issued 1985, 14" Tall.
Taffy is a sweet, blonde curly haired clown with a molded white cap sprinkled with blue flowers. She has a yellow, blue and pink striped top with pink pants. Her clown costume is trimmed with white lace and her shoes are yellow. She could be found with white, pink or green pom pons on her top. She comes in a variation of the trim being thicker than the other. The photo on the bottom left shows this variation.
Secondary Market Value: $250-275
Secondary Market Value Thicker Trim: $300-325
Purchased From _____ Date _____
Orig. S.R. $25.00   I paid $_____

Jonathan and David

D007   **Pink Missy**
               Retired – 1988
Comments: Issued 1985, 14½" Tall.
Introduced in 1985, she remained in production until J&D Company closed in 1988. Wearing a pink satin dress with the bottom part of her dress pleated, her pinafore apron varied in length, from over-lapping the pleated skirt to just meeting the pleats. People have reported "ruffles" instead of pleats on the bottom of her dress, but one may guess that the dress became wrinkled and, during an ironing session, the pleats were transformed into gathered ruffles. J&D's Missy has a "chubby" face, so a different mold was used for the PMC Pink Missy. She can be readily identified by her J&D doll tag.
Secondary Market Value: $200-250
Purchased From _____ Date _____
Orig. S.R. $28.00   I paid $_____

D008   **Blue Missy**
               Retired – 1988
Comments: Issued 1985, 14½" Tall.
Introduced in 1985, she remained a very popular doll. Except for her blue dress, she is exactly like Pink Missy, with the same variations in her white pinafore. Her doll tag will quickly identify her. Without a name tag, one would have to compare her with the PMC Missy to verify the changes in her head mold.
Secondary Market Value: $225-275
Purchased From _____ Date _____
Orig. S.R. $28.00   I paid $_____

D009   **Patti with Goose**
               Retired – 1991
Comments: Issued 1988, 16" Tall.
Two of the most popular characters in the Precious Moments collection, Patti and her loveable little goose came individually packaged, yet, they were not sold separately. Patti is not considered complete without her. Subtract $40-50 for Patti without her goose.
Secondary Market Value: $200-250
Purchased From _____ Date _____
Orig. S.R. $28.00   I paid $_____

Chapel Exclusives

1027   Coleenia
Limited to One Year of Production

Comments: Issued 1991, 16" Tall.
Coleenia was a little lady who visited the Precious Moments Chapel just before she was called home to be with the Lord. Her stepfather returned to the Chapel and shared with Sam Butcher how much her Precious Moments figurines and her visit to the Chapel meant to her. Inspired by the Lord, Sam Butcher felt that Coleenia needed to be portrayed in the Chapel's main mural, "Hallelujah Square." Mr. Butcher designed this doll as a little angel in her heavenly robe, holding a clown doll. This is a story of God's love - no beginning and no end - it only becomes greater and stronger as time goes on. Coleenia is also a Precious Moments® figurine by Enesco available as a Chapel Exclusive.
Secondary Market Value: $300-350

Purchased From _____ Date _____
Orig. S.R. $45.00   I paid $_____

1039   Chapel Fan Doll - Caucasian

Comments: Issued November, 1992, 16" Tall.
Dressed in a beige and rosebud print pinafore and layers of beige eyelet lace on her sleeves and pantaloons, she is ready to let everyone see her fan. "I'm a Precious Moments Fan" is written across her beige and mint green fan. Her puffed bow and the top of her blonde tresses match her pinafore. The mint green heart on each sleeve matches the pretty sash around her waist.
Secondary Market Value: Current

Purchased From _____ Date _____
Orig. S.R. $50.00   I paid $_____

*I am Alpha and Omega,
the beginning and the end, the first and the last.
Revelation 22:13*

Chapel Exclusive

1040   Chapel Fan Doll - African American
Comments: Issued November, 1992, 16" Tall.
This African-American darling is dressed in a beige print pinafore with beige eyelet lace, layered to accent her pantaloons and the sleeves of her blouse. Her pigtails are tied with puffed mint green bows that match the green heart on the outer edge of her shoes. The fan she holds says it all, "I'm a Precious Moments fan."
Secondary Market Value: Current
Purchased From _____ Date_____
Orig. S.R. $50.00   I paid $_____

1055   Daniel - Shepherd of the Hills
Comments: Issued 1994, 16" Tall.
Daniel was designed exclusively for the Precious Moments Chapel Shop at Shepherd of the Hills in Branson, MO. He may be purchased at the Shepherd of the Hills Gift Shop or he may be ordered through the Precious Moments Gift Catalog. He is ready to watch his sheep and keep the stray ones with his staff. He is dressed in a dark green shepherd's coat over his brown gown. His woven sash is multi-colored and his brown molded sandals match his gown. (One may assume that this picture with Daniel wearing a golden brown gown is a prototype.)
Secondary Market Value: Current
Purchased From _____ Date_____
Orig. S.R. $40.00   I paid $_____

1058   Chapel Indian Doll
Limited – 200
Comments: Issued 1994, 16" Tall.
This Chapel Indian Doll was not given an official name, and was only available through the Chapel catalog. The collectors named her, "Chapel Indian." She is dressed in a light grey leather dress which has leather strips threaded through turquoise, silver and maroon beads. On the left side of her head, she has a very beautiful turquoise feather, which is held in place by a silver design.
Secondary Market Value: $450-495
Purchased From _____ Date_____
Orig. S.R. $80.00   I paid $_____

Chapel Exclusive

1075   Bess with Map
Comments: Issued 1994, 16" Tall.
Bess is named for the late Bess Truman. The doll is holding a map to show her the way to the Precious Moments Chapel in Carthage, MO. She is dressed in a very pretty peach print dress which is accented with eyelet lace. She is wearing matching bows on her pigtails and another bow on top of her head. Her blue molded shoes have white hearts on them.
Secondary Market Value: Current
Purchased From _____ Date_____
Orig. S.R. $35.00   I paid $_____

1084   Maureen
Comments: Issued 1997, 16" Tall.
This Sweetheart doll is dressed in a lovely, white satin gown with a cascade of hearts on the skirt. Heart-shaped buttons adorn the front of the bodice and the cuffs of the sleeves. She is dressed like the Sweetheart series doll, Hannah, but differs in having black hair, brown eyes and light brown skin.
Secondary Market Value: Current
Purchased From _____ Date_____
Orig. S.R. $50.00   I paid $_____

1095   PM Collector Doll
Comments: Issued May, 1995, 16" Tall.
Dressed to enjoy life, this Precious Moments collector is wearing a comfortable pair of blue jeans with a heavenly pink sweatshirt. In the middle of her shirt are two angels on a cloud sending the message, "Love Goes On Forever." She also has a name tag. "Hello: my name is..." Like every seasoned collector, she has a blue tote bag over her shoulder, just in case she buys a few more figurines in the Precious Moments Chapel Gift Shop. A pale yellow tennis hat adorns her curly brunette hair.
Secondary Market Value: Current
Purchased From _____ Date_____
Orig. S.R. $40.00   I paid $_____

Chapel Exclusive

1097   Colette
Comments: Issued June, 1996, 16" Tall.
Looking to heaven, little four-year old Colette wanted her mother to tell her about the rainbow in the sky. Her mother explained that it is a symbol representing a promise from God. As she grew up, she always shared this wonderful news with others. Colette is dressed in a rainbow of pastel hues of pink, yellow, green and blue. She wants to represent God's promise in everyone's doll collection.
Secondary Market Value: Current
Purchased From _____Date_____
Orig. S.R. $45.00   I paid $_____

It was inspiring to listen to artist Sam Butcher describe his vision at the 1995 Chapel Christmas Celebration. Two beautiful children highlighted the special event. Dustin and Lindsay's outfits were designed by Mr. Butcher. They reflected an aura as they walked the Avenue of Angels and then lit the Christmas candle. They led the procession to the Chapel where everyone joined in singing Christmas carols. It was a silent night which turned into a holy night as folks left with the knowledge that a special blessing had been received.
                                                                                                        Jan

1102   Lindsay
Limited Edition – 750
Comments: Issued 1995, 16" Tall.
Lindsay coordinates with the angels that surround her as she is dressed in an elegant white brocade full length gown. She wears a matching bonnet.
Secondary Market Value: Current
Purchased From _____Date_____
Orig. S.R. $100.00   I paid $_____

1103   Dustin
Limited Edition – 750
Comments: Issued 1995, 16" Tall.
Dustin is dressed from head to toe in a royal outfit of white brocade and satin. His light brown hair is cut in the traditional Precious Moments boyish hair style.
Secondary Market Value: Current
Purchased From _____Date_____
Orig. S.R. $65.00   I paid $_____

Chapel Exclusive

1946   Lindsay
Limited Edition – 2,000
Comments: Issued 1995, 12" Tall.
The 12" Lindsay is a replica of the 16" doll. Her white brocade gown retains all the details of the original design. The people who attended the Chapel's Christmas Celebration were given the 12" Lindsay.
Secondary Market Value: Current
Purchased From _____ Date_____
Orig. S.R. $60.00   I paid $_____

1947   Dustin
Limited Edition – 2,000
Comments: Issued 1995, 12" Tall.
The 12" Dustin is a replica of the 16" doll. In his prince-like white brocade suit, Dustin will carry the memories of the 1995 Christmas Celebration. He was given to each person who attended the event.
Secondary Market Value: Current
Purchased From _____ Date_____
Orig. S.R. $45.00   I paid $_____

9001   Jamie
Comments: Issued 1994, 16" Tall.
This adorable brunette bunny won everyone's heart because her hair was not the traditional blonde. She is sporting a very pretty, pale yellow bunny outfit and was known to hop out of the Chapel's Gift Shop quite rapidly.
Secondary Market Value: $200-225
Purchased From _____ Date_____
Orig. S.R. $40.00   I paid $_____

---

*A man's gift maketh room for him,
and bringeth him before great men.
Proverbs 16:16*

Chapel Exclusive

See Above Photo

4th of July
Comments: Issued 1996, 7" Tall.
Secondary Market Value Blonde: $30-35
Secondary Market Value Tan: $30-35
Secondary Market Value Red: $40-50
Purchased From _____ Date_____
Orig. S.R. $10.00   I paid $_____

☐ ☐ ☐

See Above Photo

4th of July
Comments: Issued 1996, 9" Tall.
Secondary Market Value Blonde: $35-45
Secondary Market Value Tan: $35-45
Secondary Market Value Red: $50-60
Purchased From _____ Date_____
Orig. S.R. $15.00   I paid $_____

☐ ☐ ☐

Blond Casey
Limited Edition – 200
Comments: Issued 1991, 16" Tall.
Dressed in his blue and white striped uniform, Casey has his baseball mitt on and is ready to play baseball for the Precious Moments baseball team. Casey has blond hair and blue eyes.
Secondary Market Value: $200-250
Purchased From _____ Date_____
Orig. S.R. $35.00   I paid $_____

☐

Precious Moments Company Exclusive Doll

Nina
Limited to 30 Dolls
Comments: Issued 1993, 16" Tall.
In 1993, the Precious Moments Company included an offer to register for a drawing for a special doll found in the doll catalog. Nina, a very pretty brunette doll, wearing a rosebud print dress, was designed by Sam. Names were drawn in December, 1993, and thirty doll collectors were happily surprised by starting 1994 as a proud owner of Nina.
Secondary Market Value: $1,200-1,500
Purchased From _____ Date_____
Orig. S.R. Not Applicable   I paid $_____

Jan's Family

Jan & John Kropeneck
Above left:
Wendy, Jan's daughter, makes sure the Navy dolls are wearing accurate uniforms and has researched the American Indian dolls.
Below left:
Jan with son, Bill, first grandson and daughter, Cindy.
Above right:
Jan's daughter, Cindy, with husband, Jim.

Every grandchild needs a few Precious Moments to welcome him/her into the family.

Sam Butcher holding Jan's granddaughter, Brittany, with her mother, Bonnie.

General Line

1001   Jessi
Comments: Issued February, 1989, 16" Tall.
Every bride is beautiful and Jessi is no exception. She is named after one of Sam Butcher's granddaughters. Dressed in her white satin and lace gown, she is ready to give her hand to Jonny. She carries a bouquet of pastel flowers that match the dainty flowers crowning her veil.
Secondary Market Value: Current
Purchased From _____ Date _____
Orig. S.R. $50.00/$52.00   I paid $_____

1002   Patti with Goose
Retired – May, 1991
Comments: Issued December, 1989, 15" Tall.
Patti and her little goose are two of the most popular characters in the Precious Moments collection. Patti's little friend is made of soft vinyl. Patti and her goose remained unchanged during her relocation from Jonathan & David Company to Precious Moments Country. Subtract $40-50 for Patti without her goose.
Secondary Market Value: $150-200
Purchased From _____ Date _____
Orig. S.R. $40.00   I paid $_____

1003a   Missy - pink
Revised – 1990, see 1003b
Comments: Issued 1989, 15" Tall.
The mold of her head changed from that of the Jonathan & David Missy to give her a thinner face. She wore the same pink satin dress and white pinafore. She continued to have a pleated ruffle around the bottom of her dress, but her doll tag changed to a white tag reading "Missy" on the front.
Secondary Market Value: $175-195
Purchased From _____ Date _____
Orig. S.R. $35.00   I paid $_____

General Line

1003b   Missy - pink
           Retired – 1995
Comments: Issued 1990, 15" Tall.
This pink Missy is easily identified by the striped weave in her pinafore. When one has "so many children" it is not surprising that one could be somewhat overlooked. Knowing Mr. Butcher, he would be quite upset that even one Precious Moments doll was overlooked from the history of Precious Moments. Missy, for some reason, never showed up for any of her photo sessions! Her retail price increased in 1993 to $37.50 and then to $40.00 prior to retirement.
Secondary Market Value: $100-125
Purchased From _____ Date _____
Orig. S.R. $35.00/$40.00   I paid $_____

1092   Missy – Second Edition
Comments: Issued 1995, 15" Tall.
This is the second change in the original pink Missy, although the first change was only in her pinafore. Missy has let her hair down and she has put on a very pretty pink party dress to attend a wedding at the new Wedding Chapel in the Precious Moments complex. Missy has a very simple, but beautiful, pink satin ribbon in her hair, one at her waistline and one little bow on each of her white shoes. She will cheer up anyone any day of the week.
Secondary Market Value: Current
Purchased From _____ Date _____
Orig. S.R. $40.00   I paid $_____

1004   Missy - blue
          Retired – June, 1990
Comments: Issued 1989, 15" Tall.
Missy was so excited when she left Grand Rapids, Michigan, she did not bother to change her dress or pinafore. By the time she arrived in Carthage to live with the Butcher family, she had lost her chubby cheeked face. She was given her very own tag with "Missy" on the front of it.
Secondary Market Value: $175-195
Purchased From _____ Date _____
Orig. S.R. $35.00   I paid $_____

General Line

In 1989, artist Sam Butcher wanted to express his love of the Ozarks, as he readily identified with the humble beginnings of these wonderful folks. A note of caution: Annie and Andy should not be put in direct sunshine or artificial lighting, as their hair tends to turn lighter. Annie is much more difficult to locate on the secondary market.

1009   Ozark Annie
Retired – October, 1992

Comments: Issued September, 1989, 14½-15" Tall. Ozark Annie was first an exclusive through the Chapel Gift Shop. Within a few months, she was available to retail dealers. She first came without a tag and had pigtails. Shortly thereafter, she had a white tag and she was sporting braids. She was later given a miniature catalog tag. She is now difficult to find on the secondary market.
Secondary Market Value with pigtails: $200-225
Secondary Market Value with braids: $180-195
Purchased From _____ Date _____
Orig. S.R. $45.00   I paid $_____

1010   Ozark Andy
Retired – October, 1992

Comments: Issued September, 1989, 14-14¾" Tall. Andy, pictured above, was originally introduced through the Chapel Gift Shop. He measured 14¼" and came with shoulder length red hair. His face was smaller than the later model pictured left. His overalls originally came up to his neckline but later changed to show the front of his shirt. The denim changed and pant cuffs became deeper on the later model. Andy was released to retail dealers in 1990.
Secondary Market Value shoulder length hair: $175-195
Secondary Market Value shorter length hair: $145-175
Purchased From _____ Date _____
Orig. S.R. $45.00   I paid $_____

General Line

1011   Jonny
Retired – January, 1992
Comments: Issued December, 1989, 16" Tall.
Dressed in a brown tuxedo, cream colored satin shirt and a very pale yellow puffed bow tie, Jonny is ready for the ceremony to begin. Although it cannot be seen in this photo, his cummerbund matches his satin tie and yellow rose boutonniere.
Secondary Market Value: $95-120
Purchased From _____ Date _____
Orig. S.R. $45.00   I paid $_____

_____

1011   Jonny
Retired – December, 1996
Comments: Issued 1992, 17" Tall.
This was the first 17" doll produced by Precious Moments Company. His tuxedo was changed to dark grey and his shirt was changed to white satin with three shiny black stud-like buttons on the front. His puffed bow tie, cummerbund, and boutonniere changed to a pale lavender. Retail price increased in 1995 to $48.00.
Secondary Market Value: $80-95
Purchased From _____ Date _____
Orig. S.R. $45.00/$48.00   I paid $_____

_____

1011   Jonny
Comments: Issued 1997, 17" Tall.
Jonny maintained his height of 17" and only his tuxedo changed to black.
Secondary Market Value: Current
Purchased From _____ Date _____
Orig. S.R. $48.00   I paid $_____

_____

My son, forget not my law; but let thine heart keep my commandments: For length of days, and long life, and peace, shall they add to thee.
Proverbs 3:1-2

General Line

1012   Jenny
Retired – April, 1992

Comments: Issued 1990, 14³/₄"-15¹/₂" Tall.
Jenny was introduced in her ecru christening gown and bonnet with accents of bright, baby pink satin ribbons. The eyelet lace on the tiers of her gown have ecru stitching around "off white" flowers. She has a pale wine colored lace on the hem of her petticoat and panties. In 1992, her height varied from 14³/₄"-15¹/₂" and she did not have the date on the back of her neck. Her bright pink ribbons changed to pale pink and the floral design in her gown changed. Her petticoat and panties were trimmed with ecru lace. Her face tended to be a chubby square face but it later changed to an oval face.

Secondary Market Value: $200-225

Purchased From _____ Date _____

Orig. S.R. $50.00   I paid $_____

1013   Jordan
Retired – April, 1992

Comments: Issued 1990, 14³/₄"-16" Tall.
Jordan measured 14³/₄"-15¹/₂" in the beginning, but later became 16" tall. He wore a christening dress and his bonnet did not have the girlish ruffle around his face. His clothing was trimmed with pale blue satin ribbons. His underskirt and panties were trimmed with pale wine colored lace, but later changed to ecru lace. The satin ribbons changed to a brighter baby blue and the eyelet design of his gown changed.

Secondary Market Value: $175-195

Purchased From _____ Date _____

Orig. S.R. $50.00   I paid $_____

Whosoever therefore shall humble himself as this little child,
the same is greatest in the kingdom of heaven.
And whoso shall receive one such little child in my name receiveth me
Matthew 18:4-5

General Line

1014   Tiffany
Retired – July, 1995
Comments: Issued March, 1990, 16" Tall.
Like a breath of spring air, Tiffany gracefully walks into everyone's heart like a true Southern Belle. She is dressed in a beautiful, deep rose calico dress and woven bonnet. Her bonnet and the three tiers of her dress are accented with green satin ribbons and ecru lace. Her two pigtails are adorned with dainty little roses and she wears a pearl locket.
Secondary Market Value: $150-175
Purchased From _____ Date _____
Orig. S.R. $50.00   I paid $_____

___

1015   Girl Clown – Pajama Bag
Suspended – 1995
Comments: Issued 1990, 22" Tall.
This sweet girl clown has already found her place in the nursery of little girls' rooms and the doll collections of avid clown collectors. Dressed in a pink and white clown suit and stocking hat, she doesn't mind being stuffed with pajamas or tissue paper, as she wants to make everyone happy. She has had several price changes. Originally $22, the retail increased to $25 in 1991. In 1993, the retail increased to $30.
Secondary Market Value: $45-50
Purchased From _____ Date _____
Orig. S.R. $22.00/$30.00   I paid $_____

___

1017   Timmy the Angel – Caucasian
Suspended – January, 1992
Comments: Issued March, 1990, 16" Tall.
Timmy is dressed in his angelic robe of white, accented with pale yellow satin ribbon. With a golden halo and molded sandals on his feet, he is ready to step off the clouds and into the arms of collectors. Timmy is the Chapel's Leading Angel, or should I say "Mascot"? ☺
Secondary Market Value: $175-195
Purchased From _____ Date _____
Orig. S.R. $36.00   I paid $_____

16

General Line

1017a   Timmy the Angel – blue with blanket
Suspended – December, 1994
Comments: Issued January, 1992, 16" Tall.
Dressed in his heavenly blue gown, Timmy holds his security blanket. After watching the video "Timmy's Gift," and seeing him drop the little crown out of the clouds, we are assured he knows God, and that his little blanket will help him find the crown.
Secondary Market Value: $125-150
Purchased From _____ Date _____
Orig. S.R. $37.50   I paid $_____

1018   Boy Clown – Pajama Bag
Suspended – 1993
Comments: Issued 1991, 22" Tall.
Everyone loves a clown and he is the perfect place to hide a slingshot or a frog, along with a pair of pajamas. He is dressed in a pale blue and yellow clown suit and stocking cap.
Secondary Market Value: $25
Purchased From _____ Date _____
Orig. S.R. $25.00   I paid $_____

1020   Princess Sincere
Limited Edition – 10,000
Retired January, 1993
Comments: Issued October, 1990, 16" Tall.
At one time, she was a candidate to be the first "Classic" doll, as she met the criteria for the Classic Doll line – numbered, limited edition and extremely high quality. Though she is not a Classic Doll, she has become one of the most sought after. Mr. Butcher designed her to have blue beads in her headband and necklace. Unfortunately, blue beads were not available in the Philippines. Therefore, a big hunt went on in the Ozarks to locate the blue beads. Within the beautiful medallion is the thunderbird, a symbol which means, "Sacred Bearer of Happiness Unlimited." Issued in 1990, retailers did not receive her until 1991.
Secondary Market Value: $475-500
Purchased From _____ Date _____
Orig. S.R. $100.00   I paid $_____

General Line

1021   Morning Star
Comments: Issued October, 1990, 16" Tall.
A beautiful squaw, dressed in genuine leather, carries her papoose on her back. Original suggested retail increased in 1995 to $90.00.
Secondary Market Value: Current
Purchased From _____ Date _____
Orig. S.R. $75.00/$90.00   I paid $_____

1022   Casey
           Suspended – 1996
Comments: Issued July, 1991, 16" Tall.
He is the first lad to be introduced with black hair. The first 1,000 dolls had blue eyes, thereafter, his eyes were brown. Casey is proud to be on the Precious Moments baseball team in his blue and white striped uniform accented with red! When he gets up to bat, all he can say is, "Lord, I'm coming home!" Retail price increased in 1993 to $37.50 and to $40.00 in 1995.
Secondary Market Value: $95-120
Secondary Market Value Blue Eyes: $175-195
Purchased From _____ Date _____
Orig. S.R. $35.00/$40.00   I paid $_____

1023   Bethany
           Suspended – 1995
Comments: Issued November, 1991, 16" Tall.
She was the first doll with light brown skin to be introduced in the 16" doll line collection. This beautiful little lady is dressed in a pink, aqua and white floral dress which is gracefully trimmed with beautiful lace. She has a pink locket, and she knows that you will notice her white satin rosettes in her hair and the big floral print bow on the top of her head. Retail price increased in 1993 to $45.00.
Secondary Market Value: $90-95
Purchased From _____ Date _____
Orig. S.R. $40.00/$45.00   I paid $_____

General Line

1024 Colin
Suspended – 1996

Comments: Issued November, 1991, 16" Tall.
Colin is named after one of Sam Butcher's grandchildren. He is dressed in light blue pants and a pastel plaid shirt and cap which coordinates with Katie's outfit. Before his suspension, his outfit became a brighter blue and the pastel plaid became slightly more vivid. Retail prices increased in 1993 to $37.50, and again in 1995 to $40.00.
Secondary Market Value: $70-80
Purchased From _____ Date _____
Orig. S.R. $35.00/$40.00   I paid $_____

1025 Katie
Retired – September, 1996

Comments: Issued November, 1991, 16" Tall.
Katie has a big plaid bow on her pink jumper, a white with pink polka dot blouse and a plaid, wide brimmed hat to protect her blonde hair from the sun. She is named after one of Sam Butcher's granddaughters. In later production, the pink color became a brighter strawberry pink and included her pink and white saddle shoes. Her outfit coordinates with her cousin's outfit. Retail price increased in 1993 to $37.50 and again in 1995 to $40.00.
Secondary Market Value: $75-90
Purchased From _____ Date _____
Orig. S.R. $35.00/$40.00   I paid $_____

1026 Kerri
Suspended – July, 1993

Comments: Issued July, 1991, 16" Tall.
Kerri is dressed in a very cute outfit of pastel stripes and a pink long sleeved blouse. She has a pink bow on the top knot of her black hair which accentuates her innocence. She is named after one of Sam Butcher's granddaughters. In 1993, her retail price increased to $37.50.
Secondary Market Value: $80-95
Purchased From _____ Date _____
Orig. S.R. $35.00/$37.50   I paid $_____

19

General Line

1031   Sandy – blue
Suspended – December, 1994
Comments: Issued April, 1992, 16" Tall.
This very pretty blonde is dressed in a royal blue cap and gown. Her gown is trimmed in gold. She has two blue bows holding her hair in place so Mom and Dad can see that special smile on her face when she accepts that well-earned diploma. In 1993 price increased to $45, but returned to $40 in 1994.
Secondary Market Value: $80-95
Purchased From _____ Date _____
Orig. S.R. $40.00   I paid $_____

1032   Sandy – Caucasian
Comments: Issued April, 1992, 16" Tall.
She is exactly the same doll as Sandy – blue, except she is wearing a white cap and gown. She knows this is the day she has been waiting for and thinks of the precious memories she has to take into her future. Retail price increased to $45 in 1993, but returned to the $40 original price in 1994.
Secondary Market Value: Current
Purchased From _____ Date _____
Orig. S.R. $40.00   I paid $_____

1035   Philip
Retired – December, 1994
Comments: Issued October, 1992, 16" Tall.
Debbie (Butcher) Cho did an exquisite portrayal of her brother, who was loved by everyone. He is dressed in a "patched" calico shirt and jeans, with a slingshot hanging out of his back pocket, denim sneakers and two angel wings that took him home to be with the Lord. Philip's tortoise shell glasses were always sliding down his nose, because he continually laughed. The first shipment of 2,000 dolls arrived with Philip wearing sunglasses, but further shipments had clear glasses.
Secondary Market Value Sunglasses: $200-250
Secondary Market Value Clear glasses: $120-150
Purchased From _____ Date _____
Orig. S.R. $50.00   I paid $_____

General Line

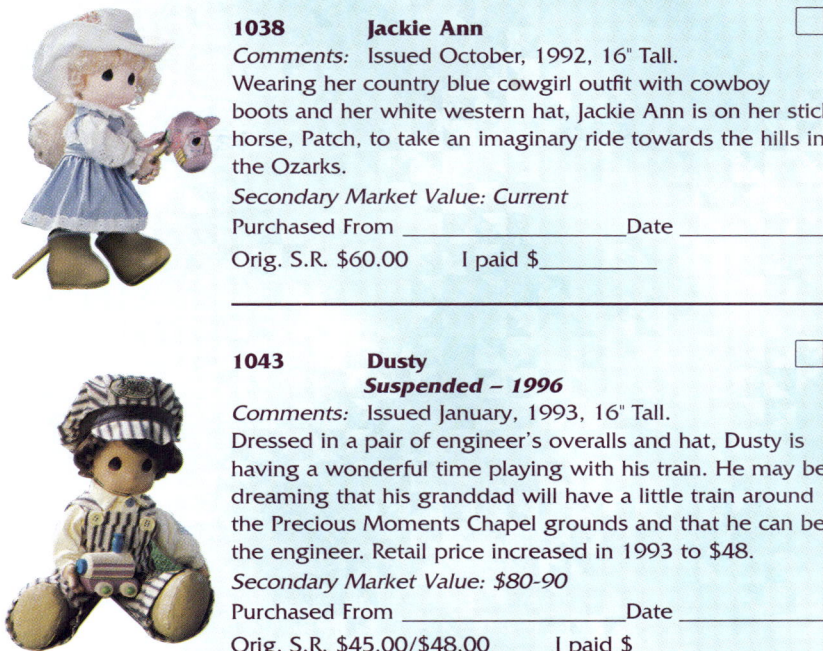

1038   Jackie Ann
Comments: Issued October, 1992, 16" Tall.
Wearing her country blue cowgirl outfit with cowboy boots and her white western hat, Jackie Ann is on her stick horse, Patch, to take an imaginary ride towards the hills in the Ozarks.
Secondary Market Value: Current
Purchased From _____ Date _____
Orig. S.R. $60.00   I paid $_____

1043   Dusty
Suspended – 1996
Comments: Issued January, 1993, 16" Tall.
Dressed in a pair of engineer's overalls and hat, Dusty is having a wonderful time playing with his train. He may be dreaming that his granddad will have a little train around the Precious Moments Chapel grounds and that he can be the engineer. Retail price increased in 1993 to $48.
Secondary Market Value: $80-90
Purchased From _____ Date _____
Orig. S.R. $45.00/$48.00   I paid $_____

1046   Delaney
Comments: Issued July, 1997, 16" Tall.
Delaney is a precious doll dressed in a red plaid dress with matching tam. She carries a basket of apples to her mother, Dawn, who is a staff member at the Precious Moments Company.
Secondary Market Value: Current
Purchased From _____ Date _____
Orig. S.R. $45.00   I paid $_____

To re-mold a doll's straw hat (for example, a hat similar to Tiffany's found on page 16 or Katie's found on page 19) first start with clean hands to make sure finger prints will not be left on the hat. With moistened fingertips, gently dampen the straw until it becomes soft and pliable and then reshape the hat.

General Line

1047 Tracey
Comments: Issued May, 1993, 16" Tall.
Tracey is dressed in her #9 pink and white striped baseball uniform, just waiting to catch a fly ball with her baseball glove. In the beginning, Tracey had a bobbed hair style. In 1994, her hair style was changed to be curly but her uniform remained the same. There were 3,500 of these dolls produced. With this variation her suggested retail price was increased to $37.50, then later to $40.00 in 1995. The third Tracey produced has her hair changed back to the original bobbed hair style. Her uniform and shoe colors have been changed to a bright raspberry pink instead of the original light pink color. Her retail price remains $40.00.
Secondary Market Value First Tracey: $95-100
Secondary Market Value Second Tracey: $80-95
Secondary Market Value Third Tracey: Current
Purchased From _____ Date _____
Orig. S.R. $36.00/$40.00   I paid $_____

See Photos Above

1048 Milly and Her New Baby Doll
Suspended – 1993
Comments: Issued September, 1993, 16" Tall.
Dressed in a pink dotted dress with blue dotted sleeves, Milly is happily surprised to find her new doll has a dress that matches hers. Of course, Milly is being the little mother, wearing a dotted swiss apron. Milly is hoping that she and her baby will be able to happily surprise many little and big girls on some special occasion. Retail price increased to $60.00 in 1995.
Secondary Market Value: $90-100
Purchased From _____ Date _____
Orig. S.R. $55.00/$60.00   I paid $_____

General Line

1057   **Dawn and Rag Doll**
Suspended – 1996
Comments: Issued June, 1993, 16" Tall.
Dawn is dressed in her pretty blue and cream colored night gown with her night cap on her head. She has her favorite rag doll with her, and will happily sing to her baby until she goes to sleep. She would be even happier sitting on some little girl's bed. Retail price increased to $60.00 in 1995.
Secondary Market Value: $90-100
Purchased From _____ Date _____
Orig. S.R. $55.00/$60.00   I paid $_____

1062   **Viola**
Comments: Issued 1996, 16" Tall.
Viola is dressed in a violet and pink floral dress with a matching hair ribbon tied around her head. Viola loves her new leather-like shoes that coordinate with her dress. She's hoping to find some violets to take to her grandmother. Her grandmother told her that God made violets to color people's lives with joy.
Secondary Market Value: Current
Purchased From _____ Date _____
Orig. S.R. $40.00   I paid $_____

1063   **Nicholas**
Limited Edition – 15,000
Comments: Issued 1993, 16" Tall.
Known as the Second Edition of Nicholas, he wears the original doll tag with a sticker over the writing stating "Second Edition." The big question: Is it more important to have the First Edition or to have the doll which is more limited in number? (See pg. 100 for First Edition of Nicholas.)
Secondary Market Value: $150-175
Purchased From _____ Date _____
Orig. S.R. $27.95   I paid $_____

General Line

1066   White Baby
Suspended – December, 1996
Comments: Issued late 1993, 16" Tall.
This doll was first issued through the Chapel catalog, then through Precious Moments Company in 1994. This newborn baby arrived in a white gown with petite aqua polka dots and an aqua ribbon to tie at the bottom of the gown. The baby also has a matching one-piece suit under the gown and dainty white knit sock. Everyone knows a new baby wears a little cap to maintain body heat. With a soft vinyl head and sculpted hair, this baby is the perfect baby for even little ones under three years of age. Retail price was increased to $36.00.
Secondary Market Value: $60
Purchased From _____ Date _____
Orig. S.R. $30.00/$36.00   I paid $_____

1067a   Brown Baby
Suspended – December, 1996
Comments: Issued late 1993, 16" Tall.
Was first issued through the Chapel catalog and then through Precious Moments Company in 1994. Babies, brown or white, they are all precious. This baby is dressed exactly like the "White Baby" and has the same soft vinyl head and sculpted hair. Retail price was increased to $36.00.
Secondary Market Value: $60
Purchased From _____ Date _____
Orig. S.R. $30.00   I paid $_____

1067b   African-American Baby
Limited Edition – 500
Comments: Issued April, 1997, 16" Tall.
This baby has dark skin and wears the same white gown with aqua polka dots as the other babies. Although the baby carries the same product number as the Brown Baby, with "Brown Baby" on the tag, it is a very limited doll.
Secondary Market Value: Current
Purchased From _____ Date _____
Orig. S.R. $36.00   I paid $_____

General Line

1068 Evie
Suspended – December, 1995
Comments: Issued 1994, 16" Tall.
She is dressed in a black skirt, red cummerbund and white blouse, with a pretty black bow and red rose adorning the top of her tresses. Evie is ready to present a large golden snowflake to anyone who loves her enough to take her home.
Secondary Market Value: $60-70
Purchased From _____ Date _____
Orig. S.R. $44.00   I paid $_____

1074 Sarah
Comments: Issued 1996, 16" Tall.
Sarah knows that God makes all things beautiful and her beauty comes from within. She is dressed exactly like the other women in her Amish village, with simple black dress, a white dress cover and her white bonnet. She knows her purpose is to touch other people's lives with her presence.
Secondary Market Value: Current
Purchased From _____ Date _____
Orig. S.R. $40.00   I paid $_____

1080 Little Mistletoe
Suspended – 1996
Comments: Issued 1995, 16" Tall.
Appearing to almost look like a Christmas clown, Mistletoe is dressed in a red and white striped suit with white pom pons down the front. He is wearing a red, green and white print stocking cap. He is ready to love and snuggle with loving girls and boys at bedtime.
Secondary Market Value: $50-55
Purchased From _____ Date _____
Orig. S.R. $32.00   I paid $_____

General Line

1085   Grandma Martha
Comments: Issued 1996, 16" Tall.
Grandma is wearing her vegetable and flower print dress and her pretty green and white coat. She wears her beloved gardening hat that she's had for many years. She has her specs on to see not only the weeds she needs to pull, but to also see God's beauty in her garden. She fills her watering can half full of water and the second half is filled with love.
Secondary Market Value: Current
Purchased From _____ Date _____
Orig. S.R. $60.00   I paid $_____

1086   Ellie
Comments: Issued 1995, 16" Tall.
Dressed in pink floral print and eyelet dress, Ellie has her hat on and is ready to go with her friends for a concert in the park. She's waiting for an invitation to be a part of someone's doll collection, or to just be loved.
Secondary Market Value: Current
Purchased From _____ Date _____
Orig. S.R. $45.00   I paid $_____

1089   Colleen
Comments: Issued 1995, 16" Tall.
Not only will Irish eyes be smiling, but so will many other eyes when Colleen enters their home. Wearing a dark green, floral print jumper and a dainty white blouse, she loves her new lace stockings and her black leather-like shoes. Her beautiful red tresses fall gracefully down her back. One does not have to wait for St. Patrick's Day to invite her to be a part of the household!
Secondary Market Value: Current
Purchased From _____ Date _____
Orig. S.R. $45.00   I paid $_____

General Line

1094   Margaret
Comments: Issued April, 1996, 16" Tall.
Dressed in a navy blue vest, green, navy, red and white plaid pleated skirt and a white blouse, Margaret holds her ABC book in her hand. Her mother tied a pretty new blue ribbon in her hair, and she wears ankle socks and molded navy shoes. Margaret knows she would be a nice reward to many little girls who bring home a report card filled with As and Bs.
Secondary Market Value: Current
Purchased From _____ Date _____
Orig. S.R. $45.00   I paid $_____

1100   Gracie
Limited to One Year of Production
Comments: Issued 1996, 16" Tall.
Gracie is a very special doll and designed after a very special young lady whose name is Gracie Blue. Her father is Rev. Royal Blue, who played the most important role in Sam Butcher's life as he lead him to the Lord. He continues to be Sam's prayer warrior and confidante. Gracie is dressed in a blue printed dress with matching blue shoes. Proceeds from the sales of the Gracie doll are being given towards Rev. Blue's ministry.
Secondary Market Value: Current
Purchased From _____ Date _____
Orig. S.R. $45.00   I paid $_____

1104   Gramma's Sweetie
Comments: Issued 1996, 16" Tall.
Collectors who purchased this doll are able to name her what they wish. My doll is named Brittany. Gramma sent her a new outfit and she can hardly wait to board the train to Gramma's house. She already has her train ticket! The first 1,000 dolls had hats and dresses made from navy tricot. Thereafter, the material has was changed to cotton.
Secondary Market Value first 1,000: $80-95
Secondary Market Value: Current
Purchased From _____ Date _____
Orig. S.R. $45.00   I paid $_____

General Line

1107   Piper
Comments: Issued April, 1997, 16" Tall.
Piper is ready to capture everyone's heart as she begins her dance. Only a few dolls were released with a net skirt touching the shoes. The most current production of Piper has a shorter tutu so her pale pink panties show.
Secondary Market Value: Current
Purchased From _____Date _____
Orig. S.R. $40.00   I paid $_____

1108   Caucasian Baby
Comments: Issued 1997, 16" Tall.
Our precious little baby is now wearing a new outfit of white with pink rosebud print. The baby has a matching cap to the sleeper and, under the gown, a one-piece jumpsuit with a white yoke accented by an applique cluster of roses. This doll will give little hands hours of pleasure learning how to dress and undress the baby.
Secondary Market Value: Current
Purchased From _____Date _____
Orig. S.R. $38.00   I paid $_____

1109   Hispanic Baby
Comments: Issued 1997, 16" Tall.
This is the first Hispanic doll to be introduced by Precious Moments Company. Baby has a soft vinyl head with reddish sculpted hair. This may be a prototype doll and may not come with this hair coloring.
Secondary Market Value: Current
Purchased From _____Date _____
Orig. S.R. $38.00   I paid $_____

1114   Pat
Comments: Issued 1997, 16" Tall.
Pat is wearing a long floral dress. She has brown shoulder length hair and is holding a pink embroidery hoop. Personalization instructions are included.
Secondary Market Value: Current
Purchased From _____Date _____
Orig. S.R. $45.00   I paid $_____

General Line

1117 **African-American Baby**
Comments: Issued 1997, 16" Tall.
This is the second African-American baby doll to be produced within a few months of each other. She makes a perfect baby gift to decorate a nursery and she will patiently wait for her "little mother" to grow to be able to hug and kiss her. Baby's outfit is the same as the Caucasian Baby and Hispanic Baby outfit.
Secondary Market Value: Current
Purchased From _____ Date _____
Orig. S.R. $38.00   I paid $_____

1118 **Grandpa Bill**
Comments: Issued 1997, 16" Tall.
Grandpa Bill is wearing his favorite straw hat, grey pants, white shirt and burgundy sweater. He has on his eyeglasses to read a Precious Moments newspaper tucked under his arm.
Secondary Market Value: Current
Purchased From _____ Date _____
Orig. S.R. $45.00   I paid $_____

1412 **Guardian Angel**
Comments: Issued 1996, 12" Tall.
Everyone needs a Guardian Angel, and this "little blessing" can fill that need nicely!
Secondary Market Value: Current
Purchased From _____ Date _____
Orig. S.R. $28.50   I paid $_____

1421 **Blonde Bride**
1422 **Blond Groom**
Comments: Issued 1997, 12" Tall.
The bride is wearing a white satin and lace wedding gown. The groom, of course, is dressed in a black tuxedo, a white satin shirt with black stud buttons and a purple tie.
Secondary Market Value: Current
Purchased From _____ Date _____
Orig. S.R. $28.50 ea. I paid $_____

General Line

1439   Angela
Comments: Issued 1996, 12" Tall.
Clasping her hands together, Angela is a reminder that prayer is the answer.
Secondary Market Value: Current
Purchased From _____ Date _____
Orig. S.R. $28.50   I paid $_____

___

1467   Clifford
Comments: Issued 1994, 12" Tall.
Clifford is dressed in a blue romper with a white shirt under a blue jacket. He is wearing a matching cap and carries a toy rabbit.
Secondary Market Value: Current
Purchased From _____ Date _____
Orig. S.R. $28.50   I paid $_____

___

1468   Winnie
Comments: Issued 1994, 12" Tall.
Clifford's sister, Winnie, is dressed in a floral dress and pink coat. She carries a little basket of eggs. Winnie would make a very special Easter gift!
Secondary Market Value: Current
Purchased From _____ Date _____
Orig. S.R. $28.50   I paid $_____

___

1490   Christina
Comments: Issued 1996, 12" Tall.
Christina is a blonde haired doll who would make a beautiful gift for baptism or communion.
Secondary Market Value: Current
Purchased From _____ Date _____
Orig. S.R. $28.50   I paid $_____

General Line

1491 **Grace**
Comments: Issued April, 1995, 12" Tall.
This doll makes a beautiful gift for baptism or communion.
Secondary Market Value: Current
Purchased From _____ Date _____
Orig. S.R. $28.50   I paid $_____

1492 **Bride**
1493 **Groom**
Comments: Issued April, 1995, 12" Tall.
The perfect Bride for the perfect Groom. First brunette Bride and Groom dolls produced by Precious Moments Company.
Secondary Market Value: Current
Purchased From _____ Date _____
Orig. S.R. $28.50 ea.   I paid $_____

1498 **Young Hee – Karate Girl**
Comments: Issued September, 1997, 12" Tall.
This cute little girl is wearing a white t-shirt under her white jacket. She's looking forward to showing off her black belt talent.
Secondary Market Value: Current
Purchased From _____ Date _____
Orig. S.R. $28.50   I paid $_____

1499 **Young Ho – Karate Boy**
Comments: Issued September, 1997, 12" Tall.
This Tae kwon do boy is ready for black belt competition wearing a white T-shirt under a white jacket. Young Ho is a perfect match for Young Hee.
Secondary Market Value: Current
Purchased From _____ Date _____
Orig. S.R. $28.50   I paid $_____

General Line

1550   Regina – Christmas Carolers ☐
Comments: Issued 1996, 9" Tall.
Regina is a sweet little blonde, dressed in a full length red dress with a lace collar. Her favorite carol is "O, Holy Night."
Secondary Market Value: Current
Purchased From _____ Date _____
Orig. S.R. $21.00   I paid $_____

1551   Natalie – Christmas Carolers ☐
Comments: Issued 1996, 9" Tall.
Dressed in a beautiful poinsettia print dress, Natalie loves to sing, "Away In the Manger" as it is the first Christmas song she learned in Sunday School.
Secondary Market Value: Current
Purchased From _____ Date _____
Orig. S.R. $21.00   I paid $_____

1552   Ian – Christmas Carolers ☐
Comments: Issued 1996, 9" Tall.
Dressed in a red plaid shirt and long green pants with gold buttons on the sides, Ian loves to sing, "Silent Night" as the gentle snowflakes fall from Heaven's open doors.
Secondary Market Value: Current
Purchased From _____ Date _____
Orig. S.R. $21.00   I paid $_____

1554   Graduate ☐
Comments: Issued April, 1997, 9" Tall.
This pretty little blonde graduate will graduate from the dealer to the collector quite quickly. Although she is not part of the Children of the World, I'm sure the children of the world are inviting her to join them.
Secondary Market Value: Current
Purchased From _____ Date _____
Orig. S.R. $21.00   I paid $_____

General Line

1708   Heather
Comments: Issued May, 1990, 16" Tall.
This adorable blonde curly-haired doll is named after Sam Butcher's youngest daughter. Her bunny bonnet, suit and booties are removable. When the dolls were first introduced the booties were not removable, therefore, one can identify this doll with or without a tag. In the beginning, she had a miniature doll catalog tag, but in 1993 she began wearing her own personal tag.
Secondary Market Value: Current
Purchased From _____ Date _____
Orig. S.R. $40.00   I paid $_____

1709   Josh
Retired – 1991
Comments: Issued May, 1990, 16" Tall.
Dressed in a blue bunny outfit, Josh has the same hair style as the other boys in the Precious Moments Company doll collection. His booties were not removable in the beginning, but later the booties could be removed.
Secondary Market Value: $150-160
Purchased From _____ Date _____
Orig. S.R. $40.00   I paid $_____

1722   Jeremy
Comments: Issued 1994, 16" Tall.
Jeremy has a white bunny outfit which is removable. He has the ability to hop into someone's arms anytime of the year!
Secondary Market Value: Current
Purchased From _____ Date _____
Orig. S.R. $40.00   I paid $_____

When giving a doll or a teddy bear to a child, remember to give it with love. That means you must not let your values such as "mint condition" or its monetary value influence the child. For if you do, you have not given the doll away. I hope my granddaughter, Brittany, will have precious moments with all the dolls I give her to play with, to create precious memories of Nana's love – Jan.

Twenty-six Inch General Line Dolls

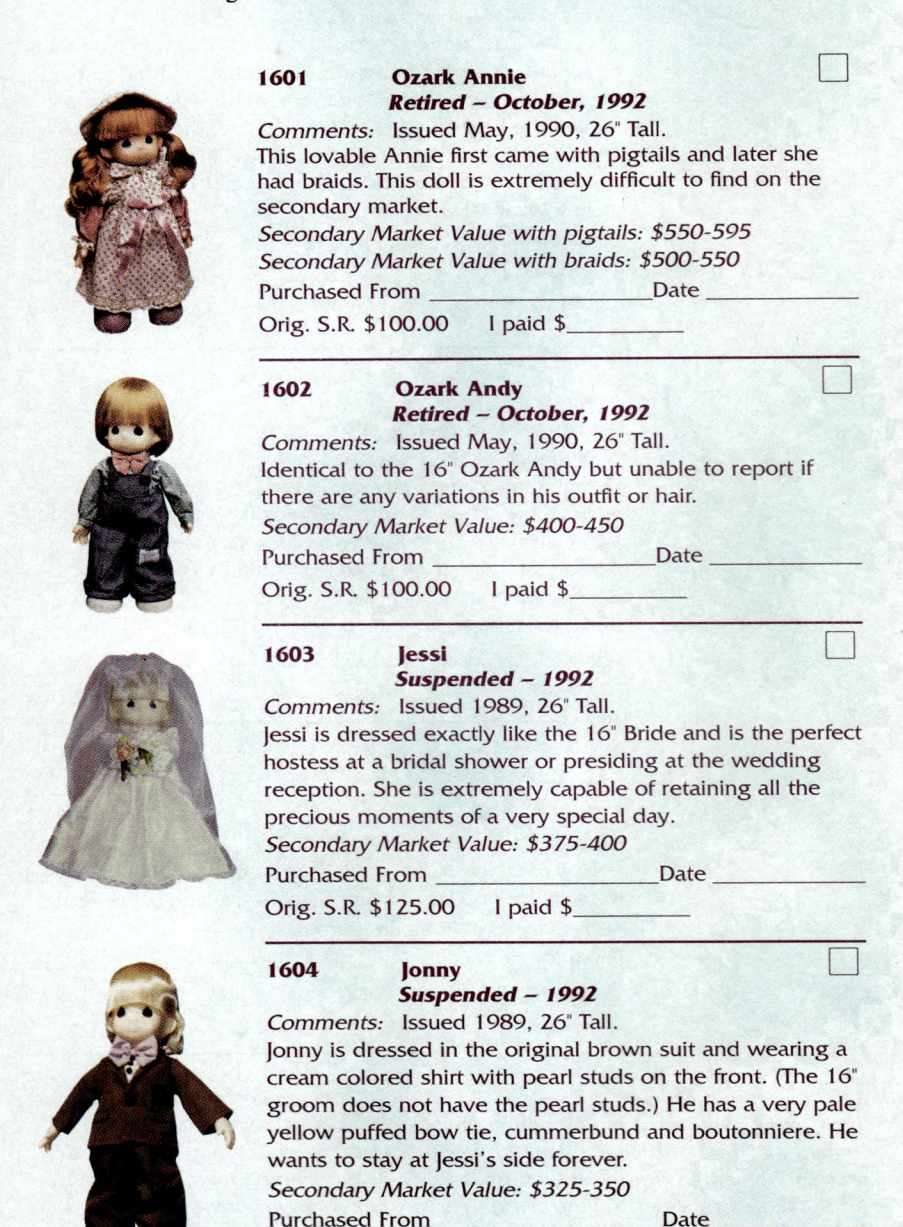

1601   **Ozark Annie**
Retired – October, 1992
Comments: Issued May, 1990, 26" Tall.
This lovable Annie first came with pigtails and later she had braids. This doll is extremely difficult to find on the secondary market.
Secondary Market Value with pigtails: $550-595
Secondary Market Value with braids: $500-550
Purchased From _____ Date _____
Orig. S.R. $100.00   I paid $_____

1602   **Ozark Andy**
Retired – October, 1992
Comments: Issued May, 1990, 26" Tall.
Identical to the 16" Ozark Andy but unable to report if there are any variations in his outfit or hair.
Secondary Market Value: $400-450
Purchased From _____ Date _____
Orig. S.R. $100.00   I paid $_____

1603   **Jessi**
Suspended – 1992
Comments: Issued 1989, 26" Tall.
Jessi is dressed exactly like the 16" Bride and is the perfect hostess at a bridal shower or presiding at the wedding reception. She is extremely capable of retaining all the precious moments of a very special day.
Secondary Market Value: $375-400
Purchased From _____ Date _____
Orig. S.R. $125.00   I paid $_____

1604   **Jonny**
Suspended – 1992
Comments: Issued 1989, 26" Tall.
Jonny is dressed in the original brown suit and wearing a cream colored shirt with pearl studs on the front. (The 16" groom does not have the pearl studs.) He has a very pale yellow puffed bow tie, cummerbund and boutonniere. He wants to stay at Jessi's side forever.
Secondary Market Value: $325-350
Purchased From _____ Date _____
Orig. S.R. $110.00   I paid $_____

Preferred Doll Retailers

See Photos Above

15000	Jessi
15010	Jonny
	Never Produced

Comments: Issued 1991, 26" Tall.
These animated dolls were produced for a flier. There are no known sales of these dolls to any dealers, although several collectors would like to have them in their collections now! These two dolls were on display at Rosie's Convention.
Purchased From _____ Date _____
Orig. S.R. $600.00 ea.   I paid $_____

Preferred Doll Retailers

1034   Amy
Limited Edition – 4,000
Comments: Issued May, 1992, 16" Tall.
This precious doll is dressed in a pink, floral print dress with pale blue and white pinafore. The puffed bows on her braids match the pinafore. Amy holds a framed message, "Precious Moments never end when shared with my forever friend." She wears pantaloons of eyelet material.
Secondary Market Value: $175-195
Purchased From _____ Date _____
Orig. S.R. $45.00   I paid $_____

35

Preferred Doll Retailers

1036 **Katlyn**
Limited to One Year of Production
Comments: Issued 1994, 16" Tall.
Wearing a pastel, floral print blouse, pale lavender and white print skirt, Katlyn has not had time to remove her eyelet apron after making a batch of cookies. She has a jar of cookies for anyone who welcomes her into their Precious Moments doll collection.
Secondary Market Value: $140-160
Purchased From _____ Date _____
Orig. S.R. $45.00   I paid $_____

1045 **Cara**
Limited to One Year of Production
Comments: Issued 1993, 16" Tall.
Dressed in a pink and green floral print dress accented with a pink collar and pink ruffles at the wrists and hem, Cara is ready to be a friend. Unfortunately, Cara had a "bad hair day" and she was recalled. The wise collector kept her and those who returned her probably regret it, as everyone knows, "bad hair days" don't last forever.
Secondary Market Value: $150-175
Purchased From _____ Date _____
Orig. S.R. $45.00   I paid $_____

1051 **Little Sunshine**
Limited Edition – 5,000
Comments: Issued 1996, 16" Tall.
Dressed somewhat similar to her big sister, Sunshine, this sweetie pie reflects God's love with the sunflowers on her headband, dress and shoes. In her black and white checkered dress and eyelet lace, she hopes that she will be invited into someone's friendship garden to add another ray of sunshine.
Secondary Market Value: Current
Purchased From _____ Date _____
Orig. S.R. $50.00   I paid $_____

Preferred Doll Retailers

1081 Robin
Limited to One Year of Production
Comments: Issued 1995, 16" Tall.
Robin wants everyone to know that Spring has arrived and her red breasted, feathered friend wants to sing a song. She wears an adorable blue and pink floral coat-dress with blue and pink plaid, long-legged pants. With a big blue silk flower holding back the brim of her pink hat, Robin is ready to brighten someone's life.
Secondary Market Value: $75-80
Purchased From _____ Date _____
Orig. S.R. $50.00   I paid $_____

1106 Lacey
Limited Edition – 3,500
Comments: Issued 1997, 16" Tall.
Feeling like a princess in a rose printed dress, Lacey loves the elegant mauve and white lace that borders the lower part of her skirt. Dainty pink satin ribbons have been woven in and out of the lace. The neckline and wrists of her blouse are also accented by the dainty ribbons. Best of all, her grandmother gave her a brooch that she wore as a little girl.
Secondary Market Value: Current
Purchased From _____ Date _____
Orig. S.R. $55.00   I paid $_____

See
Photos
Above

1445 Sara and Kara
Limited Edition
Comments: Issued 1997, 12" Tall.
Secondary Market Value: Current
Purchased From _____ Date _____
Orig. S.R. $50.00   I paid $_____

37

Preferred Doll Retailers

1605   **Sunshine**
Limited Edition – 450
Comments: Issued 1994, 26" Tall.
She'll warm your heart and put a smile on your face as she radiates sunshine from head to toe. Her black and white checkered dress has sunflowers printed on it and she loves her eyelet apron effect, which is really the skirt of her dress. Her blonde ponytail has been neatly hidden under her straw hat which also sports more sunflowers. Even her black shoes have sunflowers adorning them. Sold out.
Secondary Market Value: $950-1,000
Purchased From _____ Date _____
Orig. S.R. $150.00   I paid $_____

1606   **Maggie**
Limited Edition – 1,000
Comments: Issued 1995, 26" Tall.
It's a big day for Maggie; it is the first time she is leaving the farm to visit her cousin in the city. Her mother made her a pretty pink calico and blue plaid dress which is trimmed with eyelet lace. Her long-legged bloomers and her dust cap match her dress. Her mother was very creative by making Maggie's shoes and shoulder bag out of burlap. Maggie on the left wears her original outfit. Maggie on the right, had her outfit lovingly made by Lyn Schmidt, who wanted her to have a new dress to wear to the Chapel.
Secondary Market Value: $250-275
Purchased From _____ Date _____
Orig. S.R. $150.00   I paid $_____

See Photos Above

38

Preferred Doll Retailers

1607   Valerie
Limited Edition – 1,000
Comments: Issued 1996, 26" Tall.
She knows ladybugs bring good luck, so she loves her pinafore dress made from ladybug and flower printed material and accented with cream and green checkered material, touched with white lace. Valerie is very proud; she has learned how to braid her own hair while her mother has brushed her beautiful brunette tresses in the back. (Book not included.)
Secondary Market Value: $225-250
Purchased From _____ Date _____
Orig. S.R. $150.00   I paid $_____

Grandchildren...
are a gift from God

Parker - 4 yrs old
You must like the Green Bay Packers, motorcycles and dirt bikes to get on his list.
Taylor - 7 yrs old
You must like baseball soccer and NASCAR racing. His motto, "Part of me wants to be good!"

Bottom of the sixth inning, three on base, two outs and losing 8-7... Bryan asked for time out to stand in the batter's box for a moment. He returned to hit a triple! Later he explained that he couldn't do it, so he took time out to pray and ask God to help him.

"Prayer Changes Things"

"Grandma's Sweetie" Brittany

The Precious Children above are the Grandchildren of Jan.

🍓 Berry Best Friends 🍓

1625   Strawberry
Comments: Issued December, 1996, 14" Tall. Having brown pigtailed yarn hair, and wearing a strawberry pink and white striped bodice and skirt, Strawberry is waiting to be loved by some little girl. She has a large strawberry printed on her apron.
Secondary Market Value: Current
Purchased From _____ Date _____
Orig. S.R. $20.00   I paid $_____

1626   Raspberry
Comments: Issued December, 1996, 14" Tall. Raspberry has light brown hair with a braid crowning the top of her head and two pink roses to accent her hair style. Her raspberry and white striped clothing matches her raspberry colored shoes. Two big raspberries are printed on her apron.
Secondary Market Value: Current
Purchased From _____ Date _____
Orig. S.R. $20.00   I paid $_____

1627   Blueberry
Comments: Issued December, 1996, 14" Tall. Blueberry is a pretty little blonde, happy to be dressed in a blueberry and white striped dress. She has several blueberries on her apron. Is it possible she visited Blueberry Hill in Oregon?
Secondary Market Value: Current
Purchased From _____ Date _____
Orig. S.R. $20.00   I paid $_____

1628   Boysenberry
Comments: Issued December, 1996, 14" Tall. Boysenberry is another cute little blonde with a satin bow added to her hair. Her ensemble includes a purple and white dress with matching purple shoes. The two boysenberries on her apron let one know what she is named.
Secondary Market Value: Current
Purchased From _____ Date _____
Orig. S.R. $20.00   I paid $_____

Birthday Wishes

1951	January's Child	☐	1957	July's Child	☐
1952	February's Child	☐	1958	August's Child	☐
1053	March's Child	☐	1959	September's Child	☐
1954	April's Child	☐	1960	October's Child	☐
1955	May's Child	☐	1961	November's Child	☐
1956	June's Child	☐	1962	December's Child	☐

Comments: Issued December, 1996, 11" Tall.
Original retail price decreased July, 1997.
Secondary Market Value: Current
Purchased From_____Date _____
Orig. S.R. $20.00/$10.00   I paid $_____

Career Series

1414   Teacher   ☐

Comments: Issued July, 1997, 12" Tall.
Dressed in a denim blue jumper and a large sleeved white blouse decorated with a bright red apple, this doll represents that very special teacher who teaches the meaning of love and understanding. Her little eyeglasses have a petite gold chain. She is the first doll in this new series. She makes a wonderful gift for any little girl or a favorite school teacher. Don't forget that mothers are also our very first teachers!
Secondary Market Value: Current
Purchased From _____Date _____
Orig. S.R. $28.50   I paid $_____

Children of the World

In 1990, the dolls in this collection were introduced at $22.50, but in 1993 the price changed to $20. Since 1995, the price has remained $21.00.

1501   Carla – America
Retired – April, 1997
Comments: Issued February, 1989, 9" Tall.
She represents our ancestors of yesteryear who toiled in the fields and helped drive the covered wagons westward. Carla is dressed in a two-tone, mauve calico dress.
Secondary Market Value: $40-45
Purchased From _____ Date _____
Orig. S.R. $22.50/$21.00   I paid $_____
_____

1502   Mazie – America
Retired – 1994
Comments: Issued February, 1989, 9" Tall.
Our African-American lady represents the women who worked without ceasing to give her children a home and schooling. Mazie is dressed in a beige and cornflower calico dress.
Secondary Market Value: $50-60
Purchased From _____ Date _____
Orig. S.R. $22.50/$21.00   I paid $_____
_____

Subscribe to Rosie's
Weekly Collectors' Gazette™

Exciting news every week on Precious Moments® Collectibles
and other fabulous collectibles!
This weekly publication is only $2 an issue
8 week minimum $16, 13 weeks $24, 26 weeks $44
1 year $84 (saves $20)
You'll Hear It Here First!

Call 1-800-445-8745
To Subscribe Today!

Children of the World

See Photos Above

1503   **Shannon – Ireland**
Comments: Issued February, 1989, 9" Tall.
This Irish lass arrived in the U.S. in 1989. Since her arrival, her flowing red hair has been trimmed and changes in her dress can be seen in the polka dot print of her dress, as well as the length of the skirt.
Secondary Market Value: Current
Purchased From _____ Date _____
Orig. S.R. $22.50/$21.00   I paid $_____

1504   **Cory – Philippines**
Retired – April, 1992
Comments: Issued February, 1989, 9" Tall.
Cory is named after former President Corazon Aquino of the Philippines, whose favorite color is yellow. With jet black hair and her yellow gown, Cory is very proud to represent the Philippines. (See pg. 104)
Secondary Market Value: $75-80
Purchased From _____ Date _____
Orig. S.R. $22.50   I paid $_____

1505   **Shonnie – American Indian**
Retired – May, 1991
Comments: Issued February, 1989, 9" Tall.
This precious little squaw is dressed in a two-piece, light tan Native American dress with red, yellow, white and black decorative bands around her head, neckline, waist and hemline of her skirt. She represents the women who know only how to work with what the Great Spirit has given, such as dyes from roots, medicine from herbs and food and clothing from animals and the earth.
Secondary Market Value: $375-450
Purchased From _____ Date _____
Orig. S.R. $22.50   I paid $_____

Children of the World

1506   Misu – Japan
Retired – 1994
Comments: Issued February, 1989, 9" Tall.
Misu is dressed in a pink and burgundy kimono. After a few years of production, dealers in Hawaii notified Precious Moments Company that the Japanese customers were somewhat concerned about Misu's kimono being folding over towards the left side. The kimono is placed in this fashion on a deceased person for the cremation ceremony. This did not inhibit the sale of the doll to the Japanese customers, but they did ask the question, "Why?" This problem was put to rest when Misu was retired.
Secondary Market Value: $100-125
Purchased From _____ Date _____
Orig. S.R. $22.50   I paid $_____

See
Photos
Above

1507   Maria – Spain
Comments: Issued January, 1990, 9" Tall.
There are two different versions of Maria. The original has a flower on her right wrist and flowers on the left side of her hair. Only a small border on her black lace is showing on the four tiers of her dress. Currently, she has a deeper border of scalloped lace and her flowers on the opposite side of her hair. Variations help make a collection unique.
Secondary Market Value: Current
Purchased From _____ Date _____
Orig. S.R. $22.50/$21.00   I paid $_____

Children of the World

1508   Gretel – Sweden
Comments: Issued January, 1990, 9" Tall.
Dressed in a long black skirt, white satin blouse and a delicate pink satin apron, she is ready to bring a touch of Sweden into your life. Gretel originally came with ankle socks; later her legs were painted white. In 1997, she is wearing white tights.
Secondary Market Value: Current
Purchased From _____ Date _____
Orig. S.R. $22.50/$21.00   I paid $_____

1509   Kari – Holland
Comments: Issued December, 1990, 9" Tall.
In 1990, Kari was introduced with pigtails that extended below her hands. The length of her hair continues to vary. Presently, her apron is 3" in length which is $1/2$" shorter than the original apron. The lace on the bottom of her apron has changed to a flower and a distinctive scallop design. The plaid, multi-colored band on her skirt has changed from $3/8$" to $1/2$". The plaid shoulder straps, plaid waist band and the plaid band on her skirt vary in color, as it comes from a rainbow plaid of red to purple. The original doll may not have a tag, or it may have a miniature catalog tag "Children of the World." (See photos above.)
Secondary Market Value for Original Doll: $45-50
Secondary Market Value: Current
Purchased From _____ Date _____
Orig. S.R. $22.50/$21.00   I paid $_____

45

Children of the World

1510   Sulu – Alaska
Retired – 1996
Comments: Issued December, 1990, 9" Tall.
Dressed in a brown fur-like outfit, Sulu hoped that someday someone would present her with a white suit. It was very difficult to play "Hide and Seek" in the snow because everyone could easily identify her brown suit.
Secondary Market Value: $50-60
Purchased From _____ Date _____
Orig. S.R. $22.50/$21.00   I paid $_____

1510a   Sulu – Alaska
Comments: Issued 1996, 9" Tall.
Sulu's wish came true, for she now wears a white suit trimmed with brown fur-like material. It is now the collector who must "Seek and Find" Sulu in her brown suit.
Secondary Market Value: Current
Purchased From _____ Date _____
Orig. S.R. $21.00   I paid $_____

1511   Ivan – Russia
Retired – 1994
Comments: Issued December, 1990, 9" Tall.
Ivan was the first boy to be introduced in the series. He is dressed in a black jacket trimmed with black and gold braiding, red pants, black boots and a black fur hat. He is just waiting for the music to start so that he can do a Russian dance.
Secondary Market Value: $95-110
Purchased From _____ Date _____
Orig. S.R. $22.50   I paid $_____

   All current dolls will carry two tags. One tag will be the doll tag which carries the doll's name. Very carefully, cut off the second tag and follow the directions to send it to Precious Moments Company. PMC will have quarterly drawings - October, January, April and July. You may be the lucky person who receives a doll. The lucky winner this past July received the 1996 Christmas Classic Doll named Star.

Children of the World

1512   Gretchen – Germany

Comments: Issued December, 1990, 9" Tall.

In 1990, she arrived from Germany with a white plume in her hat. Since that time, the plume has been discontinued. Her border on her apron remained yellow with red flowers until 1993. In 1993, the border on Gretchen's apron changed from yellow to red and the flowers became "stylized." The flower design overlapped the border and production was stopped. Gretchen now has her stylized floral print within the red border on her apron. Sometimes the bud of the flowers within the floral print face to the left and other times the design goes to the right. In 1997, Gretchen is wearing white tights.

Secondary Market Value First: $90-100
Secondary Market Value Second: $45-50
Secondary Market Value Third: Current
Purchased From _____ Date _____
Orig. S.R. $22.50/$21.00   I paid $_____

See
Photos
Above

1513   Taya – India

Comments: Issued December, 1990, 9" Tall.

Taya can be found with three variations of rick-rack trim on the sleeves and hem of her costume. The doll on the left came with a Children of the World catalog tag and was produced in 1992. The center doll was produced in 1996 and came with a suitcase picture tag. The doll on the right was produced in 1991 and did not have a tag. Many feel this adds excitement to collecting when variations such as these are discovered.

Secondary Market Value: Current
Purchased From _____ Date _____
Orig. S.R. $22.50/$21.00   I paid $_____

Children of the World

1514   Angelina – Italy
Comments: Issued 1995, 9" Tall.
Dressed in her native costume of a red skirt, white blouse and a blue and white shawl matching her head covering, Angelina is ready to go to the village festivities in the vineyards.
Secondary Market Value: Current
Purchased From _____ Date _____
Orig. S.R. $21.00   I paid $_____

1515   Hans (Ollie) – Austria
Comments: Issued 1995, 9" Tall.
Yes, God loves little boys, too! First introduced with the name Ollie, his name was changed to Hans in 1996. He is the second boy in the series. Dressed in his native costume of black lederhosen, a waist-length grey jacket and white plumage in his hat, Hans would have to take you to the Alps to view the breath-taking panoramic scene of God's handiwork.
Secondary Market Value: Current
Purchased From _____ Date _____
Orig. S.R. $21.00   I paid $_____

1516   Sophie – Poland
Comments: Issued 1995, 9" Tall.
She is dressed in a floral print skirt, white blouse and apron and a black vest accented with a satin ribbon. Sophie wears a wreath of flowers in her hair. She is ready to dance a polka in the village square.
Secondary Market Value: Current
Purchased From _____ Date _____
Orig. S.R. $21.00   I paid $_____

1517   Morning Glory – American Indian
Comments: Issued 1995, 9" Tall.
She proudly wears a feather in her headband and wears a long tan Indian gown that is accented with petite beads. She is happy to meet so many other children from around the world.
Secondary Market Value: Current
Purchased From _____ Date _____
Orig. S.R. $21.00   I paid $_____

Children of the World

1518   Pualani
First Exclusive to Hawaii
Comments: Issued 1995, 9" Tall.
This girl is dressed in her grass skirt and lei of red flowers. Although originally limited to one year of production, Pualani remains in production. She is only available in Hawaii, but can be purchased on the secondary market.
Secondary Market Value: $55-70
Purchased From _____ Date _____
Orig. S.R. $21.00   I paid $_____

1519   Freya – Denmark
Comments: Issued 1996, 9" Tall.
Wearing a dark rose dress, accented with a petite floral print collar and apron, Freya is ready to tell the other children what it is like to live in Denmark.
Secondary Market Value: Current
Purchased From _____ Date _____
Orig. S.R. $21.00   I paid $_____

1523   Ollie – Norway
Comments: Issued 1996, 9" Tall.
Ollie wears a red skirt with a white blouse and apron which are accented with lace. Ollie's Norwegian bonnet helps to keep her hair in place and her ears warm from the evening breezes. She can hardly wait to teach the other girls how to knit sweaters.
Secondary Market Value: Current
Purchased From _____ Date _____
Orig. S.R. $21.00   I paid $_____

Rosie and Hunter having fun down on the farm.

Children of the World

1524   Aisha – Africa
Comments: Issued 1996, 9" Tall.
Aisha is a beautiful doll with curly black hair. She wears a gold blouse under her multi-colored, striped wrap. The matching scarf on her head has been folded in a meticulous manner and tied on the right side. Aisha loves her gold hoop earrings and her beaded necklace that her mother gave to her before she left to come to America. Pictured above is a prototype doll.
Secondary Market Value: Current
Purchased From _____ Date _____
Orig. S.R. $21.00   I paid $_____

1525   Mei-Mei – China
Comments: Issued April, 1997, 9" Tall.
Dressed in pretty pajamas of fuschia and gold satin, Mei-Mei knows everyone will invite her to come stay with them. In China, little girls are not given dolls.
Secondary Market Value: Current
Purchased From _____ Date _____
Orig. S.R. $21.00   I paid $_____

1526   Yoim – Korea
Comments: Issued April, 1997, 9" Tall.
The top of her dress has rainbow colored stripes and her beautiful long flowing skirt has an elegant Oriental print. Yoim is hoping she will find her way into everyone's heart.
Secondary Market Value: Current
Purchased From _____ Date _____
Orig. S.R. $21.00   I paid $_____

Children of the World

1527   **Alohaloni**
             Second Exclusive to Hawaii
Comments: Issued 1996, 9" Tall.
When arriving in Hawaii, many tourists are greeted with a lei and a shout of "Aloha," which is Hawaiian for "Hello." Alohaloni reminds collectors of this tradition with the floral lei around her neck and "Aloha" in her name.
Secondary Market Value: $55-65
Purchased From _____ Date _____
Orig. S.R. $21.00   I paid $_____

1528   **Keiki-Lani – Hawaii**
Comments: Issued April, 1997, 9" Tall.
This is the first Hawaiian doll made for the continental U.S. Dressed in a beautiful print gown and wearing a crown of flowers on her head, she beckons everyone from the mainland to visit her island.
Secondary Market Value: Current
Purchased From _____ Date _____
Orig. S.R. $21.00   I paid $_____

1529   **Allison – USA**
Comments: Issued April, 1997, 9" Tall.
Dressed in a navy jumper and a red and white checked blouse, Allison is very proud of her outfit that portrays our country's national colors.
Secondary Market Value: Current
Purchased From _____ Date _____
Orig. S.R. $21.00   I paid $_____

Although a 16" vinyl doll collection of the children of the world does not formally exist, dolls from the Classic Doll Collection may satisfy the collector who wants larger dolls to represent various countries. The Native American Indian, for example, is represented by three dolls, Morning Star, Chapel Indian and Miakoda. Bridget is the sweet Irish girl, while Emma and Erich could easily represent France. Hopefully, we might see a Scottish lass or an African Princess within the Classic Doll Collection.

Christmas Classic Doll Collection

1207   Marcy
Limited Edition – 6,000

Comments: Issued May, 1993, 16" Tall.
In 1993, Marcy was the first Christmas Classic Doll to be produced. Her elegant green velvet dress and cape are accented by ecru lace and red plaid lining for her cape and underskirt of her dress. With her dark brown tresses flowing over her shoulders, she is ready to celebrate the Christmas season.
Secondary Market Value: $345-360
Purchased From _____ Date _____
Orig. S.R. $125.00   I paid $_____

1211   Stephanie
Limited Edition – 7,500

Comments: Issued 1994, 16" Tall.
Stephanie stepped out in 1994 with a smile on her face, in hopes that someone would invite her for a sleigh ride! Her blonde pigtails are decorated with red ribbons and holly. Her velvet jacket is trimmed with white faux fur. Her plaid dress stands out to let her lace petticoat show. Stephanie's hands will always be warm with her fur muff.
Secondary Market Value: $250-275
Purchased From _____ Date _____
Orig. S.R. $120.00   I paid $_____

1215   Janna
Limited Edition – 5,000

Comments: Issued July, 1997, 16" Tall.
Dressed like a winter-wonderland princess, Janna wears a beautiful white satin winter dress that is trimmed with white faux fur and accented with dainty silver cording. Her white fur-like hat is accented with holly. She is carrying a satin drawstring purse. Janna is named for the wife of Craig Schoenhals, who just happens to be the CEO of the Precious Moments Company.
Secondary Market Value: Current
Purchased From _____ Date _____
Orig. S.R. $90.00   I paid $_____

Christmas Classic, Christmas Tree Toppers, Ornaments and Decorations

1217   Gloria
Limited Edition – 7,500
Comments: Issued 1995, 16" Tall.
Gloria appears as a beautiful angel who may have stepped outside the gates of Heaven to bring peace and joy to everyone during the blessed Christmas season. Her heavenly gown is accented with shimmering ribbon and gold trim. Her smile is enhanced by her dainty pearl earrings, necklace and headband. Gold and white wings are attached with velcro. Gloria sold out quite rapidly to take her place on the secondary market.
Secondary Market Value: $195-240
Purchased From _____ Date _____
Orig. S.R. $110.00   I paid $_____

1220   Star
Limited Edition – 5,000
Comments: Issued 1996, 16" Tall.
Star is dressed in a lovely green corduroy dress trimmed with satin. Her double-breasted burgundy coat is accented with petite gold buttons. Having a plush headband decorated with holly on her head, she wears her mittens for her walk in the winter wonderland.
Secondary Market Value: Current
Purchased From _____ Date _____
Orig. S.R. $110.00   I paid $_____

Christmas Tree Toppers, Ornaments and Decorations

2001   Christy
Comments: Issued 1989, 9" Tall.
Gracing the top of the Christmas tree for years, she can also be found decorating tables and mantels over fireplaces.
Secondary Market Value: Current
Purchased From _____ Date _____
Orig. S.R. $25.00   I paid $_____

Christmas Tree Toppers, Ornaments and Decorations

2002 **Carrie**
Suspended – 1991
Comments: Issued 1989, 9" Tall.
This pretty little African-American wore the same gold and white gown as Christy. She is now on many collectors' "want" lists.
Secondary Market Value: $60-75
Purchased From _____ Date _____
Orig. S.R. $25.00   I paid $_____

___

2003 **Christie**
Discontinued
Comments: Issued 1989, 3" Diameter.
This Christmas decoration was only produced in 1989. There is a matching tree topper.
Secondary Market Value: $25-30
Purchased From _____ Date _____
Orig. S.R. $10.00   I paid $_____

___

2004 **Carrie**
Discontinued
Comments: Issued 1989, 3" Diameter.
This Christmas decoration was only produced in 1989. There is a matching tree topper.
Secondary Market Value: $25-30
Purchased From _____ Date _____
Orig. S.R. $10.00   I paid $_____

___

2005 **Timmy**
Suspended – 1995
Comments: Issued 1992, 9" Tall.
Timmy is dressed in a very simple angelic gown which is trimmed in pale yellow satin. Being a perfect angel, he has a gold halo.
Secondary Market Value: $40-60
Purchased From _____ Date _____
Orig. S.R. $25.00   I paid $_____

Christmas Tree Toppers, Ornaments and Decorations

2006   Harmony
Comments: Issued 1995, 9" Tall.
Wearing a dark green gown trimmed with ecru lace, Harmony holds a gold foil gift box decorated with gold stars. She may be a tree topper but she certainly could be the perfect accent on a table cloth.
Secondary Market Value: $35-45
Purchased From _____ Date _____
Orig. S.R. $25.00   I paid $_____

2007   Peace
Suspended – 1996
Comments: Issued 1995, 9" Tall.
This brunette angel is dressed in a beautiful burgundy gown trimmed in gold. A beautiful petite, wine colored rose adorns her gold foil gift box.
Secondary Market Value: $35-45
Purchased From _____ Date _____
Orig. S.R. $25.00   I paid $_____

2008   Joy
Comments: Issued 1995, 9" Tall.
A pretty little blonde angel will be happy wherever she is placed - on top of the tree, on the mantel or on a bedside table. Joy is dressed in an angelic white gown with gold trim. One wonders what is in the gift box as an offering to her Heavenly Father.
Secondary Market Value: Current
Purchased From _____ Date _____
Orig. S.R. $25.00   I paid $_____

2009   Gold - Angel
Comments: Issued July, 1995, 7" Tall.
This Flying Angel is a Christmas decoration.
Secondary Market Value: Current
Purchased From _____ Date _____
Orig. S.R. $20.00   I paid $_____

Christmas Tree Toppers, Ornaments and Decorations

2010 **Silver - Angel**
Comments: Issued July, 1995, 7" Tall.
This Flying Angel is a Christmas decoration.
Secondary Market Value: Current
Purchased From _____ Date _____
Orig. S.R. $20.00   I paid $_____

2011 **Angelica**
Limited Edition – 5,000
Comments: Issued 1996, 12" Tall.
In her breathtaking white satin gown, with an overskirt of tulle, Angelica is reaching out to touch everyone's heart. Her gold beaded halo and matching necklace coordinate with the gold on her gown.
Secondary Market Value: $55-60
Purchased From _____ Date _____
Orig. S.R. $30.00   I paid $_____

2015 **Celeste**
Limited Edition – 5,000
Comments: Issued July, 1997, 12" Tall.
This is the first angel tree topper who has her hands clasped in prayer. Celeste is dressed in an iridescent gold and white satin gown. She is a wonderful reminder that prayer is a perfect way to start and end the day.
Secondary Market Value: Current
Purchased From _____ Date _____
Orig. S.R. $30.00   I paid $_____

Ask us about Rosie's Midwest Collectibles Fests Held Semi - Annually. Many older dolls may often be found at this "Granddaddy of all Shows".
Call 1-800-445-8745
or
309-668-2211

Classic Doll Collection

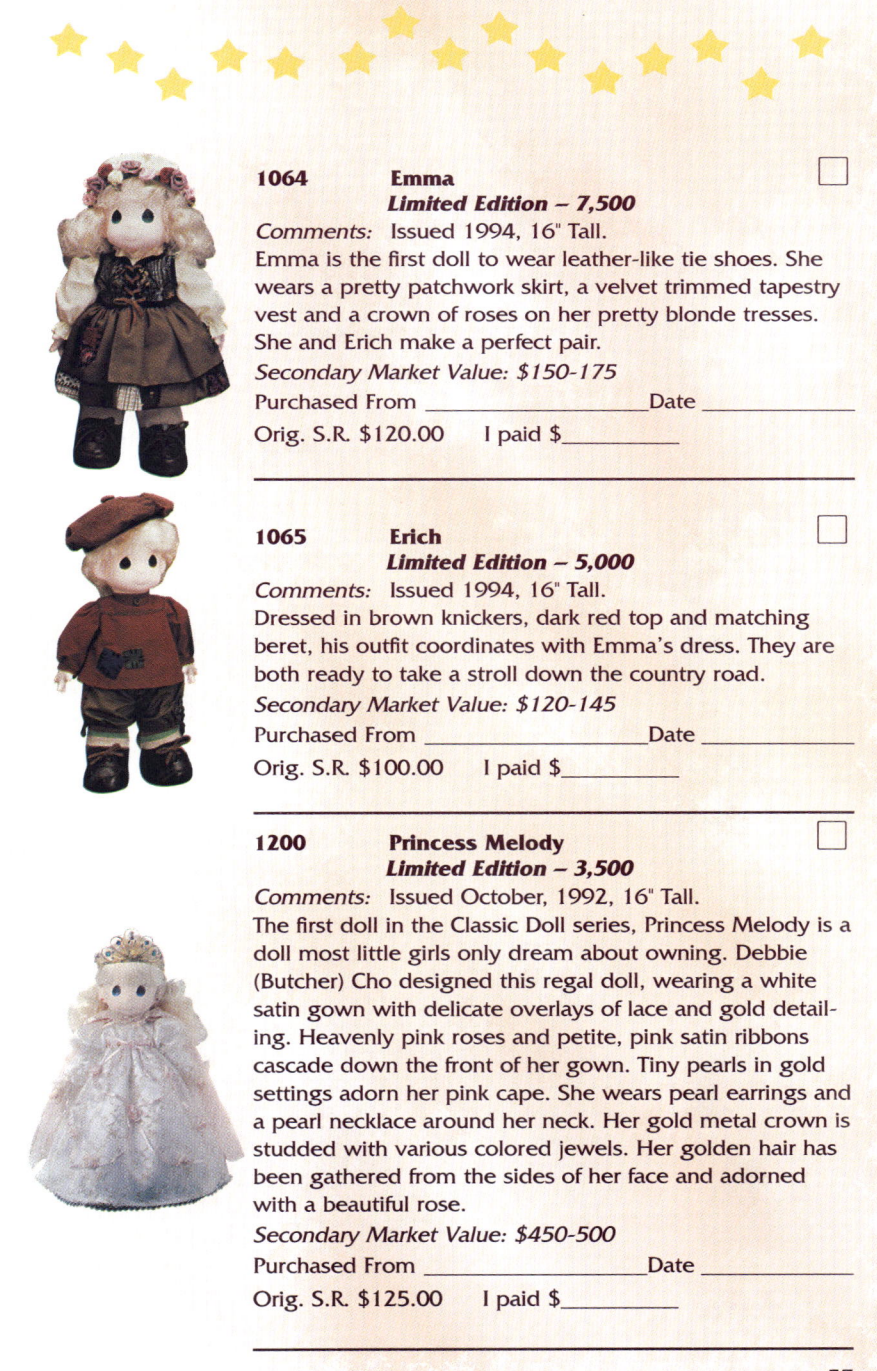

1064   Emma
Limited Edition – 7,500
Comments: Issued 1994, 16" Tall.
Emma is the first doll to wear leather-like tie shoes. She wears a pretty patchwork skirt, a velvet trimmed tapestry vest and a crown of roses on her pretty blonde tresses. She and Erich make a perfect pair.
Secondary Market Value: $150-175
Purchased From _____ Date _____
Orig. S.R. $120.00   I paid $_____

1065   Erich
Limited Edition – 5,000
Comments: Issued 1994, 16" Tall.
Dressed in brown knickers, dark red top and matching beret, his outfit coordinates with Emma's dress. They are both ready to take a stroll down the country road.
Secondary Market Value: $120-145
Purchased From _____ Date _____
Orig. S.R. $100.00   I paid $_____

1200   Princess Melody
Limited Edition – 3,500
Comments: Issued October, 1992, 16" Tall.
The first doll in the Classic Doll series, Princess Melody is a doll most little girls only dream about owning. Debbie (Butcher) Cho designed this regal doll, wearing a white satin gown with delicate overlays of lace and gold detailing. Heavenly pink roses and petite, pink satin ribbons cascade down the front of her gown. Tiny pearls in gold settings adorn her pink cape. She wears pearl earrings and a pearl necklace around her neck. Her gold metal crown is studded with various colored jewels. Her golden hair has been gathered from the sides of her face and adorned with a beautiful rose.
Secondary Market Value: $450-500
Purchased From _____ Date _____
Orig. S.R. $125.00   I paid $_____

Classic Doll Collection

1201   Melinda
Limited Edition – Less Than 7,000

Comments: Issued May, 1993, 16" Tall.
Melinda is the second doll in the Classic Doll series. Retailers had to place orders prior to her production. She was named after one of Sam Butcher's daughters-in-law. Melinda is dressed in a soft blue gown that is beautifully accented with a generous display of delicate white lace, designed to make a shawl-like collar. A big blue bow adorns her blonde tresses. She wears dainty pearl earrings and a pearl ring.
Secondary Market Value: $300-350
Purchased From _____ Date _____
Orig. S.R. $90.00   I paid $_____

1202   Andreah
Limited Edition – 6,000

Comments: Issued December, 1993, 16" Tall.
Dressed in an old-fashioned gown of pink satin and lace with smocking above the waistline, Andreah arrived in time to be given to a special loved one for Christmas. She loves the beautiful cameo that her great grandmother gave to her. Her dark brown tresses are neatly tucked under her dust cap.
Secondary Market Value: $125-150
Purchased From _____ Date _____
Orig. S.R. $75.00   I paid $_____

1210   Bridget
Limited Edition – 7,500

Comments: Issued January, 1994, 16" Tall.
Dressed in a plaid skirt, white blouse and beautiful knit cardigan sweater, hat and stockings, Bridget is ready to put down her basketful of shamrocks to dance an Irish jig. Her green Irish eyes, red hair and freckled cheeks will steal your heart away.
Secondary Market Value: $175-195
Purchased From _____ Date _____
Orig. S.R. $105.00   I paid $_____

Classic Doll Collection, Four Seasons Doll Collection

1213   Miakoda
Limited Edition – 7,500
Comments: Issued 1995, 16" Tall.
She was introduced as "Miakota" but her correct name is "Miakoda." An Apache Indian adolescent, she is dressed in her genuine leather ceremonial costume. Her beaded earrings, bracelet and necklace accent the intricate hand beading on her dress.
Secondary Market Value: $180-200
Purchased From _____ Date _____
Orig. S.R. $120.00   I paid $_____

1214   Happy
Limited Edition – 7,500
Comments: Issued 1995, 16" Tall.
Everyone loves a clown! Inspired by Mr. Butcher's figurine, "Put On A Happy Face," Happy also has a mask. He is dressed in a clown suit; half is made of gold lamé and the other side of a deep blue material sprinkled with gold stars. His collar and shoes are made of red with gold star material. Balls on his hat, bells on his toes. Happy will make you laugh, Ho, Ho, Ho!
Secondary Market Value: $160-195
Purchased From _____ Date _____
Orig. S.R. $105.00   I paid $_____

Four Seasons Doll Collection

1069   Brooke – Spring
Comments: Issued 1995, 16" Tall.
Every little girl, ages 2-90, loves a new outfit when it is springtime, and Brooke loves her new pink and yellow print dress and hat. She wears a very pretty, strawberry pink jacket and carries a little box-like purse.
Secondary Market Value: Current
Purchased From _____ Date _____
Orig. S.R. $50.00   I paid $_____

Four Seasons Doll Collection

1070   Megan – Summer
Comments: Issued 1995, 16" Tall.
In her pink and white checked blouse and her pastel, flower print coverall, Megan wears her straw hat to keep the sun out of her eyes. She's ready to play on the swings in the park. She loves her picnic lunch that Aunt Kristi gave her. Of course, by the time she arrives home the basket will be empty.
Secondary Market Value: Current
Purchased From _____ Date _____
Orig. S.R. $50.00   I paid $_____
_____

1071   Ashley – Fall
Comments: Issued 1995, 16" Tall.
Dressed in a beige blouse and a floral print skirt with hues of brown, Ashley wears a little cameo on her bow at the neckline. She loves her rust-colored hat that accents the two little braids on each side of her pretty face. She holds a basketful of grapes for her grandmother.
Secondary Market Value: Current
Purchased From _____ Date _____
Orig. S.R. $50.00   I paid $_____
_____

1072   Whitney – Winter
Comments: Issued 1995, 16" Tall.
Dressed in a berry print blouse and dark green skirt, Whitney has a gold headband and gold belt to coordinate with her gold basket filled with berries. She is hoping that she will bring happiness to many little girls throughout the year.
Secondary Market Value: Current
Purchased From _____ Date _____
Orig. S.R. $50.00   I paid $_____
_____

To remove black marks from a doll's vinyl face or hands, take a Q-tip and moisten it with Soft Scrub. It is not recommended to be used on any painted area such as eyebrows, lips, eyes or eye shadow, but it will remove black or blue marks quite nicely. Make sure to wash the area with a soft soapy cloth, rinse and dry.

Garden of Friends 1

1455   **Jasmine – January**
Limited Edition – 15,000
Comments: Issued 1994, 12" Tall.
This pretty little blonde is dressed in her winter outfit, just waiting to see if she will have to go to school or if she gets to stay home and play in the winter snow.
Secondary Market Value: $50-55
Purchased From _____ Date _____
Orig. S.R. $28.50   I paid $_____

1456   **Violet – February**
Limited Edition – 15,000
Comments: Issued 1994, 12" Tall.
Dressed in her violet print dress, Violet is happy to be holding a pot of violets for her favorite teacher. Her dark brown hair is held in place with a matching violet satin ribbon.
Secondary Market Value: $50-55
Purchased From _____ Date _____
Orig. S.R. $28.50   I paid $_____

1457   **Lily – March**
Limited Edition – 15,000
Comments: Issued 1994, 12" Tall.
Carrying a basket of flowers, Lily is dressed in a very stylish, lily-of-the-valley print jumpsuit with a mauve ruffled collar blouse. Her tan hair and face are protected from the sun by her delicate, straw woven hat which is decorated with a mauve satin ribbon and flowers. Sold out very quickly!
Secondary Market Value: $90-95
Purchased From _____ Date _____
Orig. S.R. $28.50   I paid $_____

Garden of Friends 1

1458   Daisy – April
Limited Edition – 15,000
Comments: Issued 1994, 12" Tall.
Everyone loves daisies and Daisy is no exception! This red-headed darling is thrilled with her daisy print coat and matching hat. Daisies on her hat and daisies in her hand, she's happy that spring has arrived. Sold out very quickly.
Secondary Market Value: $90-95
Purchased From _____ Date _____
Orig. S.R. $28.50   I paid $_____

1459   Iris – May
Limited Edition – 15,000
Comments: Issued 1994, 12" Tall.
May is the month for dancing around the Maypole and Memorial Day parades. Iris is dressed in her new blue and white dress with her blue shoulder bag purse. Her tan hair is held in place by her satin, periwinkle blue ribbon which coordinates with her dress and shoes.
Secondary Market Value: $90-95
Purchased From _____ Date _____
Orig. S.R. $28.50   I paid $_____

1460   Rose – June
Limited Edition – 15,000
Comments: Issued 1994, 12" Tall.
Dressed in a very dainty, rose printed dress with petite, pink satin roses and bows on her sleeves, Rose is ready to be a flower girl in a garden wedding. She has roses and satin bows in her hair and carries a basket of flowers. Sold out very quickly.
Secondary Market Value: $90-95
Purchased From _____ Date _____
Orig. S.R. $28.50   I paid $_____

Garden of Friends 1

1461   **Pansy – July**
            Limited Edition – 15,000
Comments: Issued 1994, 12" Tall.
With trowel in hand, Pansy is ready to help Grandpa in the garden. She wears an appropriate outfit of printed navy overalls and a dainty, short sleeved pink and white blouse.
Secondary Market Value: $65-70
Purchased From _____ Date _____
Orig. S.R. $28.50   I paid $_____

1462   **Blossom – August**
            Limited Edition – 13,000
Comments: Issued 1994, 12" Tall.
Blossom holds her basket filled with goodies from the garden. She wears a vegetable print jumper with a blue and white checked blouse. A straw hat with hot pink flowers adorns her blonde hair.
Secondary Market Value: $80-90
Purchased From _____ Date _____
Orig. S.R. $28.50   I paid $_____

1462   **Blossom – August**
            Limited Edition – 2,000
Comments: Issued 1994, 12" Tall.
Only Blossom's jumper changed to a flowered print; otherwise, she remained the same.
Secondary Market Value: $80-90
Purchased From _____ Date _____
Orig. S.R. $28.50   I paid $_____

Dolls that are in limited editions or exclusively made for other companies come with certificates. This would include PDR, Classic Dolls and Tree Toppers. If the doll does not have its certificate, many people hesitate to purchase on the secondary market. He who hesitates may not be able to find the doll again!

Garden of Friends 1

1463   **Sunny – September**
Limited Edition – 15,000
Comments: Issued 1994, 12" Tall.
Sunflowers always seem to reflect God's heavenly sunshine. Sunny is dressed in farm print overalls with a checked blouse. To add a little more sunshine to her life, she has put a few flowers in her pigtails and still holds a flower for her mother. Sold out very quickly.
Secondary Market Value: $95-100
Purchased From _____ Date _____
Orig. S.R. $28.50   I paid $_____

1464   **Pumpkin – October**
Limited Edition – 15,000
Comments: Issued 1994, 12" Tall.
Dressed in a brown, tan, lavender and purple print jumper over a cream colored blouse, Pumpkin has picked a bouquet of flowers for her favorite friend. She's hoping Farmer Brown will give her a pumpkin to carve for Halloween.
Secondary Market Value: $60-65
Purchased From _____ Date _____
Orig. S.R. $28.50   I paid $_____

1465   **Chrissy – November**
Limited Edition – 15,000
Comments: Issued 1994, 12" Tall.
Red-headed Chrissy is dressed up to go to Aunt Tammy's house for Thanksgiving. Her dress is printed velvet with a pretty beige collar trimmed in lace.
Secondary Market Value: $65-75
Purchased From _____ Date _____
Orig. S.R. $28.50   I paid $_____

Garden of Friends 1, Garden of Friends 2

1466   **Holly – December**
Limited Edition – 15,000
Comments: Issued 1994, 12" Tall.
Dressed in her Christmas outfit of white satin and flower print with red bows at the wrists and neckline, Holly is hoping she will make someone happy with her gift. With holly in her hair and on her red foil gift box, this precious doll knows she will make many little girls happy on Christmas morning.
Secondary Market Value: $55-60
Purchased From _____ Date _____
Orig. S.R. $28.50   I paid $_____

Garden of Friends 2

Each little girl holds a watering can with her name on it.
Limited to 17,500 of each doll.

1425   **Jasmine – January**
Comments: Issued 1996, 12" Tall.
Dressed in her new, deep lavender winter outfit, Jasmine loves her pretty rose, violet and white flower print jacket and bonnet. Her blonde hair style remains unchanged.
Secondary Market Value: Current
Purchased From _____ Date _____
Orig. S.R. $28.50   I paid $_____

1426   **Violet – February**
Comments: Issued 1996, 12" Tall.
After playing out in the garden, Violet's brunette hair is not as curly. Of course, her mother removed her dress and now she wears a violet print play outfit.
Secondary Market Value: Current
Purchased From _____ Date _____
Orig. S.R. $28.50   I paid $_____

Garden of Friends 2

1427   Lily – March
Comments: Issued 1996, 12" Tall.
Lily has changed from her mauve play outfit and is now wearing a deep rose blouse with a floral print jumper. She has also changed the satin ribbon on her hat to match her blouse.
Secondary Market Value: Current
Purchased From _____ Date _____
Orig. S.R. $28.50   I paid $_____

1428   Daisy – April
Comments: Issued 1996, 12" Tall.
Daisy loved her old coat so much that her mother made another coat out of the same material. However, the sleeves are shorter and her mother added a white collar to her coat. Her hat now has a white lining and is turned up in the front with two daisies.
Secondary Market Value: Current
Purchased From _____ Date _____
Orig. S.R. $28.50   I paid $_____

1429   Iris – May
Comments: Issued 1996, 12" Tall.
Iris decided to change her light brown hair to a darker brunette. She changed from her Sunday School dress to a pretty, white scallop collar blouse and a floral print jumper. Now she's ready to water the flowers in the backyard.
Secondary Market Value: Current
Purchased From _____ Date _____
Orig. S.R. $28.50   I paid $_____

1430   Rose – June
Comments: Issued 1996, 12" Tall.
Although she wears the same style dress, it is now deep blue. Rose has mauve roses on the sleeves of her dress and has added pink roses in her hair.
Secondary Market Value: Current
Purchased From _____ Date _____
Orig. S.R. $28.50   I paid $_____

Garden of Friends 2

1431   Pansy – July
Comments: Issued 1996, 12" Tall.
Pansy loves to play in her grandmother's garden, so she is dressed in her play clothes. She wears a new, rose colored blouse with the sleeves and collar trimmed in eyelet lace. Her little overalls are made from a pretty, pansy print material.
Secondary Market Value: Current
Purchased From _____ Date _____
Orig. S.R. $28.50   I paid $_____

___

1432   Blossom – August
Comments: Issued 1996, 12" Tall.
Blossom has changed into her Sunday best, a delft blue and white dress. She wears her lace-like straw hat to protect her blonde hair from the hot sun. Blossom loves to water the flowers in front of the church.
Secondary Market Value: Current
Purchased From _____ Date _____
Orig. S.R. $28.50   I paid $_____

___

1433   Sunny – September
Comments: Issued 1996, 12" Tall.
Her blue and white checked blouse now has short sleeves and a petite golden yellow bow at the neckline. Her girlish overalls are made from a sunflower print on dark blue. Sunny always has sunflowers in her pigtails.
Secondary Market Value: Current
Purchased From _____ Date _____
Orig. S.R. $28.50   I paid $_____

___

1434   Pumpkin – October
Comments: Issued 1996, 12" Tall.
Pumpkin has changed her jumper to a very pretty, autumn leaf print. She has added a satin bow to the neckline of her blouse.
Secondary Market Value: Current
Purchased From _____ Date _____
Orig. S.R. $28.50   I paid $_____

Garden of Friends 2, Garden of Friends 3

1435   **Chrissy – November**
Comments: Issued 1996, 12" Tall.
Chrissy's hairdo has a slight change, as her pretty auburn hair has straight bangs and her tresses are not as curly. She is now dressed in a tan floral print and pretty lace trimmed bib collar.
Secondary Market Value: Current
Purchased From _____ Date _____
Orig. S.R. $28.50   I paid $_____

1436   **Holly – December**
Comments: Issued 1996, 12" Tall.
Holly has put a black velvet, pearl-buttoned vest on to accentuate her pretty poinsettia print skirt. For her birthday, Holly received her very own watering pot with her name on it.
Secondary Market Value: Current
Purchased From _____ Date _____
Orig. S.R. $28.50   I paid $_____

Garden of Friends 3

1388   **Jasmine – January**
Comments: Issued 1997, 12" Tall.
Jasmine is wearing a dark blue velvet jumper with a white silky shirt. A blue headband holds her blonde hair. Completing her ensemble, she wears dark blue shoes and carries a pink purse.
Secondary Market Value: Current
Purchased From _____ Date _____
Orig. S.R. $28.50   I paid $_____

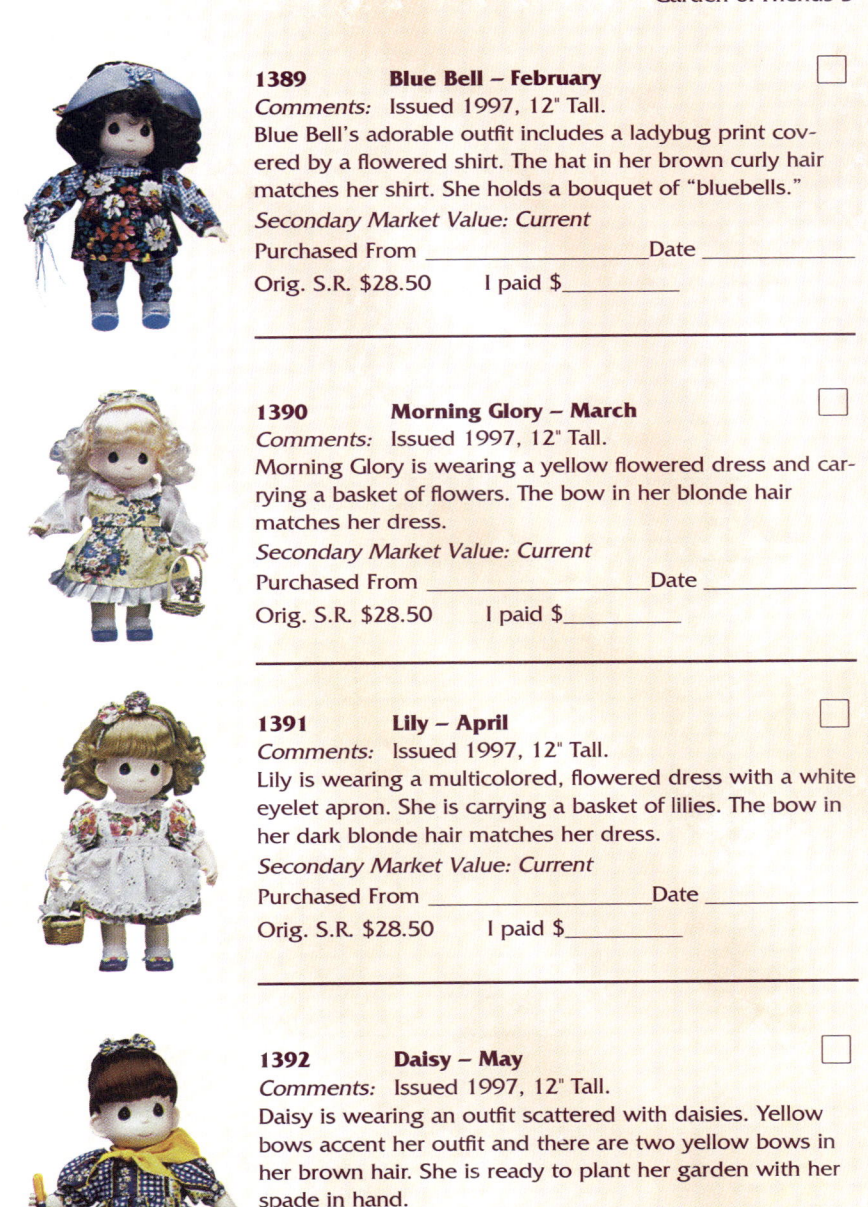

Garden of Friends 3

1389   Blue Bell – February
Comments: Issued 1997, 12" Tall.
Blue Bell's adorable outfit includes a ladybug print covered by a flowered shirt. The hat in her brown curly hair matches her shirt. She holds a bouquet of "bluebells."
Secondary Market Value: Current
Purchased From _____ Date _____
Orig. S.R. $28.50   I paid $_____

1390   Morning Glory – March
Comments: Issued 1997, 12" Tall.
Morning Glory is wearing a yellow flowered dress and carrying a basket of flowers. The bow in her blonde hair matches her dress.
Secondary Market Value: Current
Purchased From _____ Date _____
Orig. S.R. $28.50   I paid $_____

1391   Lily – April
Comments: Issued 1997, 12" Tall.
Lily is wearing a multicolored, flowered dress with a white eyelet apron. She is carrying a basket of lilies. The bow in her dark blonde hair matches her dress.
Secondary Market Value: Current
Purchased From _____ Date _____
Orig. S.R. $28.50   I paid $_____

1392   Daisy – May
Comments: Issued 1997, 12" Tall.
Daisy is wearing an outfit scattered with daisies. Yellow bows accent her outfit and there are two yellow bows in her brown hair. She is ready to plant her garden with her spade in hand.
Secondary Market Value: Current
Purchased From _____ Date _____
Orig. S.R. $28.50   I paid $_____

Garden of Friends 3

1393   **Rose – June**
Comments: Issued 1997, 12" Tall.
Rose is wearing a cream colored dress with pink roses and a matching pink shirt. She is carrying a pot of flowers and wearing a pink headband and bows in her blonde braided hair.
Secondary Market Value: Current
Purchased From _____ Date _____
Orig. S.R. $28.50   I paid $_____

1394   **Pansy – July**
Comments: Issued 1997, 12" Tall.
Pansy is wearing a pink and white checked shirt under a colorful jumper decorated with different seeds and flowers. Her pants are green and white checked and she wears a matching bow that pulls her brown hair to one side. She is carrying a nest full of eggs.
Secondary Market Value: Current
Purchased From _____ Date _____
Orig. S.R. $28.50   I paid $_____

1395   **Peony – August**
Comments: Issued 1997, 12" Tall.
Peony wears a multicolored jumper accented with pink and white checkers. She has pink and white bows that pull her brown, curly hair into pigtails. Peony holds a garden spade.
Secondary Market Value: Current
Purchased From _____ Date _____
Orig. S.R. $28.50   I paid $_____

1396   **Sunny – September**
Comments: Issued 1997, 12" Tall.
Sunny wears a dark blue dress patterned with white polka dots and sunflowers. The bow in her dark blonde hair is made from the same material as the dress. She is holding a hat in her hands.
Secondary Market Value: Current
Purchased From _____ Date _____
Orig. S.R. $28.50   I paid $_____

Garden of Friends 3

1397   Pumpkin – October
Comments: Issued 1997, 12" Tall.
Pumpkin wears a multicolored, checked dress decorated with bees and flowers. She is wearing a dark green hat with a bow of the same material as the dress in her dark brown, braided hair. She is carrying a basket.
Secondary Market Value: Current
Purchased From _____ Date _____
Orig. S.R. $28.50   I paid $_____

1398   Marigold – November
Comments: Issued 1997, 12" Tall.
Marigold wears a dark blue jacket and matching hat with her flowered yellow skirt. There are marigolds accenting her outfit on her jacket, hat and in her hand. Her hair is a beautiful red color.
Secondary Market Value: Current
Purchased From _____ Date _____
Orig. S.R. $28.50   I paid $_____

1399   Holly – December
Comments: Issued 1997, 12" Tall.
Wearing a red and green dress decorated with holly and red velvet trim, Holly wears a red and black velvet hat in her brown hair. She is holding a Christmas wreath with a big red bow on it.
Secondary Market Value: Current
Purchased From _____ Date _____
Orig. S.R. $28.50   I paid $_____

If you happen to have the privilege of having Sam Butcher sign a doll, please remember to have the body of the doll signed. Many collectors have learned from experience that having a shoe signed is somewhat heartbreaking as the ink tends to "bleed" into the molded vinyl material. Add approximately $20-$25 to the value of your doll or animal if it carries Sam's signature.

Military

1405   Army Girl
Comments: Issued January, 1997, 12" Tall.
In honor of the young women who served in the army during WWII, this gal did not mind wearing a shirt and tie like the men. She was proud to be an American who fought for freedom.
Secondary Market Value: Current
Purchased From _____ Date _____
Orig. S.R. $28.50   I paid $_____

1406   Army Boy
Comments: Issued January, 1997, 12" Tall.
This young man represents the ground troops and the Air Corps from WWII. With only a few days notice, these young men were on their way to train stations with their limited amount of personal belongings in their duffel bags. From the trains, they boarded "troop ships" with hundreds of other men, never knowing how long it would be before the war would end. Some gave their lives, but many returned home when freedom was won.
Secondary Market Value: Current
Purchased From _____ Date _____
Orig. S.R. $28.50   I paid $_____

1409   Navy Girl
Comments: Issued September, 1997, 12" Tall.
Although many of us assume the color of the uniform is navy blue, it is actually black. She is wearing her service dress uniform with cover hat.
Secondary Market Value: Current
Purchased From _____ Date _____
Orig. S.R. $28.50   I paid $_____

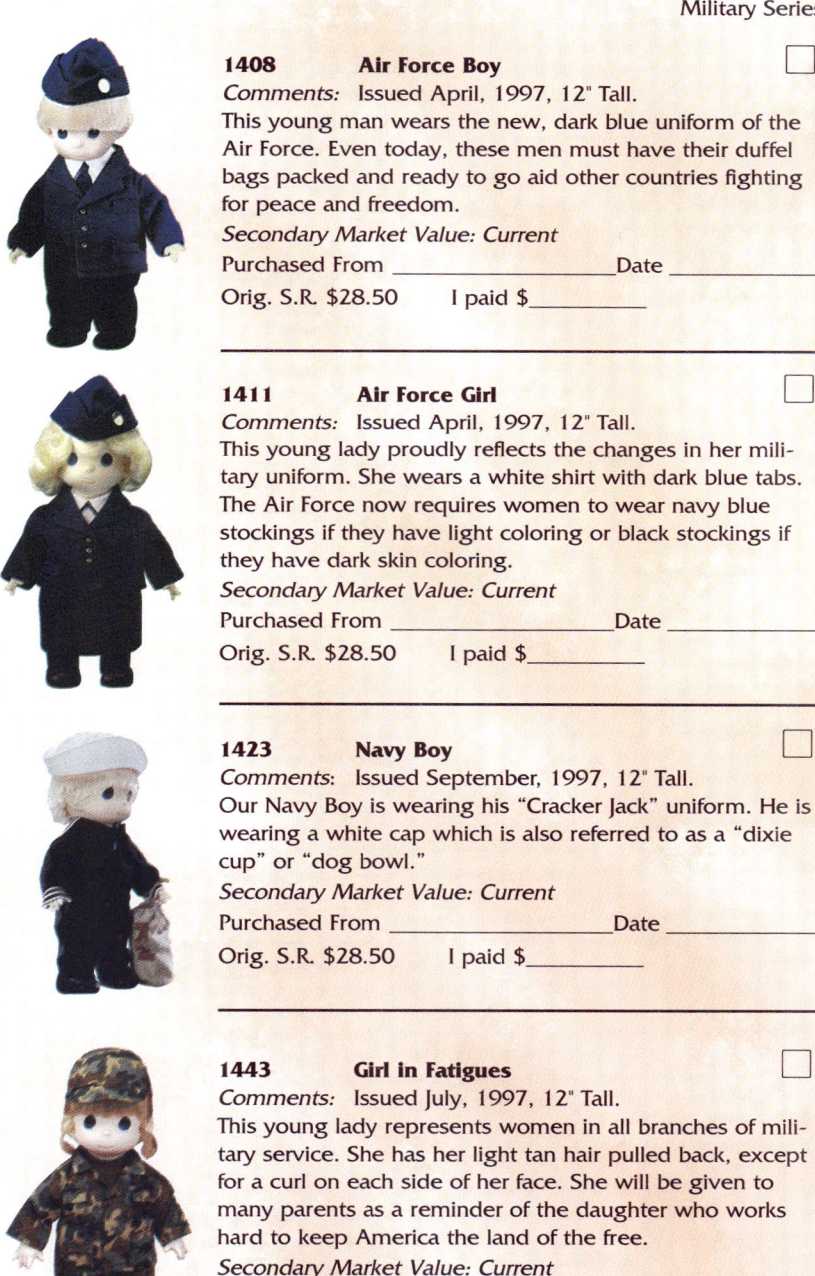

Military Series

1408   Air Force Boy
Comments: Issued April, 1997, 12" Tall.
This young man wears the new, dark blue uniform of the Air Force. Even today, these men must have their duffel bags packed and ready to go aid other countries fighting for peace and freedom.
Secondary Market Value: Current
Purchased From _____ Date _____
Orig. S.R. $28.50   I paid $_____

1411   Air Force Girl
Comments: Issued April, 1997, 12" Tall.
This young lady proudly reflects the changes in her military uniform. She wears a white shirt with dark blue tabs. The Air Force now requires women to wear navy blue stockings if they have light coloring or black stockings if they have dark skin coloring.
Secondary Market Value: Current
Purchased From _____ Date _____
Orig. S.R. $28.50   I paid $_____

1423   Navy Boy
Comments: Issued September, 1997, 12" Tall.
Our Navy Boy is wearing his "Cracker Jack" uniform. He is wearing a white cap which is also referred to as a "dixie cup" or "dog bowl."
Secondary Market Value: Current
Purchased From _____ Date _____
Orig. S.R. $28.50   I paid $_____

1443   Girl in Fatigues
Comments: Issued July, 1997, 12" Tall.
This young lady represents women in all branches of military service. She has her light tan hair pulled back, except for a curl on each side of her face. She will be given to many parents as a reminder of the daughter who works hard to keep America the land of the free.
Secondary Market Value: Current
Purchased From _____ Date _____
Orig. S.R. $ 28.50   I paid $_____

Military Series, Mommy, I Love You Series

1444   Boy in Fatigues
Comments: Issued July, 1997, 12" Tall.
This red-headed young man is ready to work anywhere for freedom and peace. He represents all branches of military service and is ready to defend his country at any time.
Secondary Market Value: Current
Purchased From _____ Date _____
Orig. S.R. $28.50   I paid $_____

Mommy, I Love You Series

1030   Janet and Baby Sarah
Limited to One Year of Production
First in Series
Comments: Issued January, 1992, 16" Tall.
Mr. Butcher dedicated this doll in memory of a very special lady who had been a nanny to one of his grandchildren. Tragically killed in a motorcycle accident, Janet Owens is greatly missed by her daughter, Sarah, and the Butcher family.
Secondary Market Value: $200-225
Purchased From _____ Date _____
Orig. S.R. $55.00   I paid $_____

1044   Jessi and Baby Lisa
Limited to One Year of Production
Second in Series
Comments: Issued January, 1993, 16" Tall.
Jessi and Jonny (Bride and Groom dolls) were more than delighted when Lisa arrived on Grandpa Sam Butcher's birthday. Jessi carries Lisa's birth certificate inside her doll tag for safe keeping. "Weight 2 $1/2$ oz., Length 7" Long."
Secondary Market Value: $180-200
Purchased From _____ Date _____
Orig. S.R. $55.00   I paid $_____

Mommy, I Love You Series

1060   **Kathy and Donnie**
Limited to One Year of Production
Third in Series
Comments: Issued 1994, 16" Tall.
In 1994, Debbie (Butcher) Cho wanted to design a mother and baby to honor her mother, Kathy, and her brother, Donnie. Kathy can't help letting a tear roll down her face, as she looks upon Donnie's precious note and drawing of her as queen. Donnie, ready for bed, still holds a yellow crayon in his left hand. Of course, his dad (Sam) is left-handed but states, "It seems right to me!" Pictured is a prototype of Donnie holding a red crayon in his right hand; there are no known dolls produced like this.
Secondary Market Value: $160-175
Purchased From _____ Date _____
Orig. S.R. $55.00   I paid $_____

1082   **Lori and Ginnie**
Fourth in Series
Comments: Issued 1995, 16" Tall.
Little Ginnie is so proud to be dressed like her mommy. She is ready to stir the cake batter with her little wooden spoon. Lori has the perfect recipe in her pocket: "Mom's Secret Recipe for Love."
Secondary Market Value: $145-160
Purchased From _____ Date _____
Orig. S.R. $60.00   I paid $_____

1101   **Susan with Twins**
Limited to One Year of Production
Fifth in Series
Comments: Issued 1996, 16" Tall.
Susan is delighted to be the first doll who presents the collector with a set of twins. She is dressed in a mauve, yellow and white floral print dress. Her mauve polka-dot top, trimmed with three pearl buttons with eyelet lace on each sleeve, is only worn to church or when friends are coming to visit. Susan has dressed her babies in yellow, as they are two rays of heavenly sunshine. She knows her strength to care for these precious babies will come only from above.
Secondary Market Value: $125-150
Purchased From _____ Date _____
Orig. S.R. $55.00   I paid $_____

Mommy, I Love You Series, Native American Dolls 1

1088   **Carissa and Baby Tess**
Limited to One Year of Production
Sixth in Series
Comments: Issued 1997, 16" Tall.
Carissa has received a wonderful Mother's Day gift, her new baby. She will always remember this day and all the days to come, as they build their precious memories together.
Secondary Market Value: Current
Purchased From _____ Date _____
Orig. S.R. $55.00   I paid $_____

Native American Dolls 1

When the Native American Dolls were first made available, it was possible to purchase all six dolls having the same edition number on the doll tags. A secondary market value of $600 would be given for a matched set of six Native American Dolls.

1482   **Zuni**
Limited Edition – 7,500
Comments: Issued 1995, 12" Tall.
This little Indian would be found in the northeastern part of Arizona and is well known for her fine work in silver and painting.
Secondary Market Value: $45-55
Purchased From _____ Date _____
Orig. S.R. $30.00   I paid $_____

1483   **Hopi Maiden**
Limited Edition – 7,500
Comments: Issued 1995, 12" Tall.
The Hopi Nation was a large and powerful tribe in the northeastern part of Arizona. Their name meant "the peaceful ones" or "all peaceful." This little Indian girl not only looks peaceful, but is very pretty in her turquoise and silver jewelry.
Secondary Market Value: $50-60
Purchased From _____ Date _____
Orig. S.R. $30.00   I paid $_____

Native American Dolls 1

1484 Yakima
Limited Edition – 7,500
Comments: Issued 1995, 12" Tall.
Yakima means "A narrow passage." Her ancestors lived along the Columbia River in Washington, but later their land was turned over to the government and they were moved to a reservation.
Secondary Market Value: $55-65
Purchased From _____ Date _____
Orig. S.R. $30.00   I paid $_____

1485 Iroquois
Limited Edition – 7,500
Comments: Issued 1995, 12" Tall.
This young squaw came from a group of Indians also known by the name of the "Five Nations" (Mohawk, Oneida, Cayuga, Seneca and the Onondaga). When the Tuscarora were added, they became known as the "Six Nations." The Iroquois were highly organized and had a strong government. Women were property owners and had the right to vote in council meetings.
Secondary Market Value: $100-120
Purchased From _____ Date _____
Orig. S.R. $30.00   I paid $_____

1486 Sioux
Limited Edition – 7,500
Comments: Issued 1995, 12" Tall.
This Native American maiden, dressed in her navy costume, represents the great Sioux Nation. Seven original tribes created the alliance which was called, "Seven Council Fires." They had three different dialects and preferred to be called by the language group. They lived mostly in South Dakota and Minnesota.
Secondary Market Value: $60-65
Purchased From _____ Date _____
Orig. S.R. $30.00   I paid $_____

1487   **Seminole**
Limited Edition – 7,500
Comments: Issued 1995, 12" Tall.
Their name means "runaway" or "the peninsula people." These people were a mixture of other tribes, such as the Yuchi, Upper Creeks and Creeks. In 1817, the first official Seminole war began and lasted for eight years. Many stayed in the Everglades (Florida), but some were moved to Oklahoma. This little squaw can be seen in her native dress in a few areas of the Everglades even today.
Secondary Market Value: $60-75
Purchased From _____ Date _____
Orig. S.R. $30.00   I paid $_____

Native American Dolls 2

These dolls were not available for sale in matching numbered sets.

1401   **Chippewa**
Limited Edition – 5,000
Comments: Issued 1996, 12" Tall.
This little squaw has her braids wrapped with leather and a silver beaded trim. Chippewa refers to her moccasins (the toes are puckered up). She is from one of the largest tribes north of Mexico and lived in the Great Lakes regions. She lived in a bark house and her people were known as great canoe men.
Secondary Market Value: Current
Purchased From _____ Date _____
Orig. S.R. $30.00   I paid $_____

Don't you think I would make a cute Precious Moments doll?!

Your old camera man from Channel 13.

John Kropenick

Native American Dolls 2

1402　　Shoshoni
Limited Edition – 5,000
Comments: Issued 1996, 12" Tall.
Shoshoni is very proud of her ancestors who lived in what is now Wyoming, Nevada and parts of Idaho. She may have lived along the Missouri River and in Montana. Her buckskin dress is beaded and she wears feathers on the ends of her two braids.
Secondary Market Value: Current
Purchased From _____ Date _____
Orig. S.R. $30.00   I paid $_____

1403　　Jacarilla Apache
Limited Edition – 5,000
Comments: Issued 1996, 12" Tall.
This young squaw would be happy to show others her fine basket work, as this is why the Apache gave her group of Indians this name. Groups in the Apache tribe were taken from features and never from animals. These nomadic people roamed the areas of Colorado, New Mexico, Kansas and Texas.
Secondary Market Value: Current
Purchased From _____ Date _____
Orig. S.R. $30.00   I paid $_____

1404　　Navajo
Limited Edition – 5,000
Comments: Issued 1996, 12" Tall.
Dressed in a pink skirt and blue top with silver accents, this little squaw's ancestors lived in Arizona and New Mexico. They were great warriors and usually won their battles against the white man. In 1849, the Navajos made peace and acknowledged the rule of the United States.
Secondary Market Value: Current
Purchased From _____ Date _____
Orig. S.R. $30.00   I paid $_____

Nativity

1555   Nativity Set
Comments: Issued July, 1997, 9" Tall.
Mary, Joseph and Baby Jesus come as a set. Mary is wearing a beige wrap around her head with a light purple veil over it. She wears a lace shawl over her coral satin robe. She depicts a wonderful lesson to every new mother that thanks be given to God for the miracle of life. Joseph is wearing a royal blue velvet cloak over his emerald green and gold robe, a gold sash around his waist and a head covering of wine velvet. Expect additional dolls and animals to be added in the coming years.
Secondary Market Value: Current
Purchased From _____ Date _____
Orig. S.R. $50.00   I paid $_____

Nursery Rhymes Series

1419   Red Riding Hood
       First In Series
Comments: Issued July, 1997, 12" Tall.
Dressed in a blue and white gingham dress and red hooded cape, Red Riding Hood is carrying a little a basket of goodies to her sick grandmother. She is the first doll in this series.
Secondary Market Value: Current
Purchased From _____ Date _____
Orig. S.R. $28.50   I paid $_____

Pearls & Lace Series

1115   Victoria
Limited Edition – 3,500

Comments: Issued July, 1997, 16" Tall.
She is the first doll in the series Pearls and Lace. Victoria, better known as Vicki Cash, editor of Chapel Bells, is wearing a very lovely, mint green chiffon and satin gown accented with pink rosette and pearls. Make sure you take your doll to the Chapel, as Vicki would be delighted to sign her.
Secondary Market Value: Current
Purchased From _____ Date _____
Orig. S.R. $52.00   I paid $_____

Plaid Rag Dolls

These little darlings may be difficult to find on the secondary market, as they make an ideal gift for little hands, or to replace a bow on a gift box.

1610   Green and Pink Plaid
Discontinued – December, 1996

Comments: Issued 1995, 7" Tall.
Dressed in a green and pink plaid skirt and vest, white blouse and petite matching plaid heart tied to her vest, this doll has short yellow yarn hair with plaid head band.
Secondary Market Value: $20-22
Purchased From _____ Date _____
Orig. S.R. $10.00   I paid $_____

1611   Red and Blue Plaid
Discontinued – December, 1996

Comments: Issued 1995, 7" Tall.
She is dressed in a black and red plaid long-legged romper. Her yellow yarn braids are adorned with blue satin bows and a plaid beret. Many folks have commented that "her heart did not come with her." Wrong, as she happens to have two hearts decorating her romper.
Secondary Market Value: $20-22
Purchased From _____ Date _____
Orig. S.R. $10.00   I paid $_____

Plaid Rag Dolls

1612 Blue and Yellow Plaid
Discontinued – December, 1996
Comments: Issued 1995, 7" Tall.
She is dressed in a dainty, powder blue, pink and white pinafore over a white blouse and skirt which are trimmed with eyelet lace. She has a red, yellow and black plaid heart with a bright yellow bow attached at her waistline. The heart matches the bow in her tan yarn hair.
Secondary Market Value: $20-22
Purchased From _____ Date _____
Orig. S.R. $10.00   I paid $_____

1613 Royal Blue Plaid
Discontinued – December, 1996
Comments: Issued 1995, 7" Tall.
She is wearing a white blouse with a long, royal blue plaid skirt. Lace trims the neckline of her blouse, sleeves, white apron and the bottom of her skirt. Her tan yarn braids are tied with kelly green satin ribbons. Green satin ribbon trims her apron pocket and holds her red plaid fabric heart around her neck.
Secondary Market Value: $20-22
Purchased From _____ Date _____
Orig. S.R. $10.00   I paid $_____

Ellen & Preston opening
PM Dolls for Christmas!

Becky L. with display case of
collectibles & PM Christmas Dolls.

Precious Jewel Dolls

Introduced in 1996, these breathtaking dolls are the first 18" dolls to be produced by Precious Moments Company. Many thousands of Precious Moments collectors will never see or hear Sam Butcher speak about God's love. Through these Jewel dolls, Sam Butcher shares his vast knowledge of the scriptures as he gains inspiration to be a vessel of God's love.

Each doll comes with a certificate of authenticity that includes a Biblical interpretation of each gem by Mr. Butcher. Many folks have sung the song "Precious Jewels" as a child. In Malachi 3:17, the Lord speaks of coming to take up his "Jewels," meaning the Lord's faithful ones.

Although these dolls are extremely beautiful, their beauty intensifies as one learns about their Biblical representation.

1221   Desert Rose
Limited to One Year of Production

Comments: Issued April, 1996, 18" Tall.

It is hard to imagine going to the desert to find such a beautiful rose. Her leather dress is decorated with beading and pink satin roses, with a rose colored feather in her headband. Her card contains this message: When the prophet Isaiah spoke of God's Blessing upon His people, Israel, He said, 'She shall blossom as a rose in the desert, (Isaiah 35:1.)

Desert Rose does not enjoy the luxuries of a manicured and watered garden. Instead, she can only wait patiently for an occasional shower from Heaven and only after that is she able to open wide her petals to the very God of her existence.

Secondary Market Value: Current

Purchased From _____ Date _____

Orig. S.R. $180.00   I paid $_____

Desert Rose tends to be the most popular doll in the Precious Jewel Doll Series due to the fact that there are so many avid collectors that seek only the American Indian Dolls.

Precious Jewel Doll Series

1222   Jade
Limited to One Year of Production

Comments: Issued September, 1996, 18" Tall.
This beautiful Oriental doll is dressed in a jade satin gown and wine-colored cape. Both garments are trimmed in gold, including the frogs on her dress.

"Jade is a mystic jewel that rests in the splendor of the Orient. Unlike rare and precious gems, she is found in abundance and, because of her size, is often prized by sculptors who carve her translucent core into a vast array of forms. Jade is a symbol of both beauty and submission. In the rough, she is unattractive and crude, but in the hands of The Master, she is transformed into statuesque grace. There is a lesson in this jewel for all who seek the utmost for God's big heart. In ourselves, we are crude and without a promise of hope. But, when we submit our lives to the Master of our soul, He will lovingly transform us into a trophy of His Grace."

Secondary Market Value: Current
Purchased From _____ Date _____
Orig. S.R. $150.00   I paid $_____

1223   Pearl
Limited to One Year of Production

Comments: Issued January, 1997, 18" Tall.
Dressed in a white satin gown, the bodice and skirt displaying a lattice design in gold, she wears a pearl over her heart.

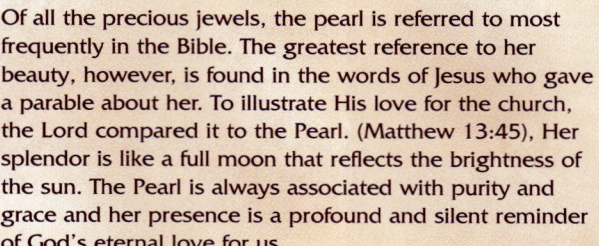

Of all the precious jewels, the pearl is referred to most frequently in the Bible. The greatest reference to her beauty, however, is found in the words of Jesus who gave a parable about her. To illustrate His love for the church, the Lord compared it to the Pearl. (Matthew 13:45), Her splendor is like a full moon that reflects the brightness of the sun. The Pearl is always associated with purity and grace and her presence is a profound and silent reminder of God's eternal love for us.

Secondary Market Value: Current
Purchased From _____ Date _____
Orig. S.R. $150.00   I paid $_____

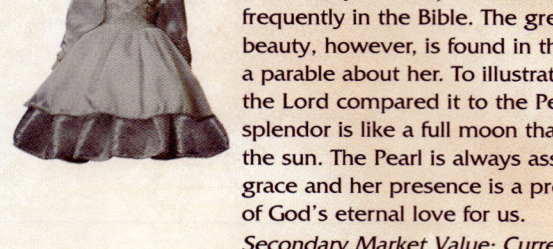

Jade has been popular among those collectors who wish to purchase a large Chinese doll. Jade is the first Chinese doll to be produced by Precious Moments Company.

Precious Jewel Doll Series

1224 Beryl
Limited to One Year of Production

Comments: Issued September, 1996, 18" Tall.
She is dressed in an elegant yellow gown with tan curled tresses cascading over her shoulders.

Beryl is adorned in a glow of warmth and yellow gold. Her name is mentioned eight times in the Bible and in every instance, she represents the perfection and holiness of God. The careful attention to every detail in the craftsmanship of Beryl makes her a unique and precious jewel that truly melts the heart of all who behold her beauty.

Secondary Market Value: Current
Purchased From _____ Date _____
Orig. S.R. $150.00   I paid $_____

1225 Ruby
Limited to One Year of Production

Comments: Issued January, 1996, 18" Tall.
She is wearing a ruby red multi-tiered gown with a matching hat.

To emphasize the value of wisdom, the Bible compares it to the Ruby, because the Ruby is so beautiful that only wisdom exceeds her beauty. 'She (wisdom) is more precious than Rubies; and all the things thou canst desire are not compared to her.' (Proverbs 3:15.) The ruby is mentioned seven times in the Bible and on each occasion, she shines forth as a masterpiece of God's wonderful gift from above.

Secondary Market Value: $200-250
Purchased From _____ Date _____
Orig. S.R. $150.00   I paid $_____

Precious Jewel Doll Series

1226   Amber
Limited to One Year of Production

Comments: Issued July, 1996, 18" Tall.
Her gown is made of amber brocade and gold lamé. Her hair is in beautiful curls which rest on her shoulders.
In his description of a Heavenly vision, the prophet Ezekiel spoke about an image that appeared as bright and as pure as amber. As he related his experience, the prophet focused his attention on the gentle glow that illuminated from the gem.
Amber is a warm unthreatening light that invokes tranquility and peace, a jewel that dazzled in a vision of a man who stood in the presence of God.

Secondary Market Value: Current
Purchased From _____ Date _____
Orig. S.R. $150.00   I paid $_____

1227   Sapphire
Limited to One Year of Production

Comments: Issued January, 1997, 18" Tall.
Sapphire is presented in a lovely sapphire gown and wears a matching bow in her hair. Her dress is trimmed with gold.
The Sapphire is a rare and precious stone that has beautified the garments of Israel and Levitical Priests and graced their temples through the ages. The Hebrew name Sapphire means "beloved one," and she is mentioned in the Bible at least eleven times.
A star appears in the star sapphire on a field of heavenly blue and her light emanates from within and speaks to each of us who trust in Christ, the bright and Morning Star, (Revelation 22:16.) Let your light shine before men that they may see your good works and glorify your Father which is in Heaven, (Matthew 5:16.)

Secondary Market Value: Current
Purchased From _____ Date _____
Orig. S.R. $160.00   I paid $_____

Precious Jewel Doll Series

1228 Crystal
Limited to One Year of Production
Comments: Issued January, 1996, 18" Tall.
Crystal is dressed in the purest white gown with five tiers of delicate beauty creating the skirt.
When the author of Revelation describes the beauty and perfection of Heaven, he said that the streets of the city are as "pure and as clear as Crystal," (Revelation 21:11.) Crystal is not considered to be a rare and precious jewel, yet she is radiantly lovely and directs the eyes of all her beholders to God, whom she reflects in every facet of her being.
Secondary Market Value: $200-250
Purchased From _____ Date _____
Orig. S.R. $150.00   I paid $_____

See Photo Above

1229 Opal
Limited to One Year of Production
Comments: Issued April, 1996, 18" Tall.
Opal is dressed in a very simplistic but elegant gown, adding her beauty to the Precious Moments doll collection.
While Opal is not mentioned in the Bible, her very name, meaning "precious stone," is a symbol of beauty and grace. Opal is a flaming field of every color known to man. Through the ages, this radiant jewel has burned her way into the hearts of all who behold the wonder of her fire.
Secondary Market Value: Current
Purchased From _____ Date _____
Orig. S.R. $160.00   I paid $_____

Precious Jewel Doll Series

1230 Jasper
Limited to One Year of Production

Comments: Issued July, 1996, 18" Tall.

Jasper is dressed in a deep, rose velvet gown with the sleeves and neckline trimmed with eyelet floral print. Her brunette hair is styled in finger curls and bangs, and the top of her hair is pulled back and adorned with the same colored bow and a rose. Her dress and bow are outlined with gold cording and a rose-colored jewel is at her neckline.

There is a beautiful promise in the Bible about Heaven, and in His description, the Lord tells us that the "first foundation of the city is made of Jasper,"(Revelation 21:18-19.) The name Jasper means "treasure holder" and, as the first foundation, what greater treasure could Jasper hold than that of a city who's builder and maker is God?

Secondary Market Value: Current

Purchased From _____ Date _____

Orig. S.R. $150.00   I paid $_____

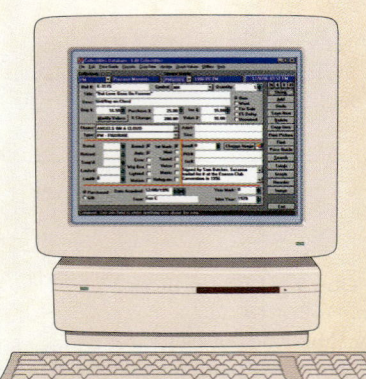

Collectibles Database™

The Best Collecting Software for Collectors.

You can stay organized using your computer!

Featuring Price Guides by Rosie Wells Enterprises, Inc.
Create insurance reports, inventory lists, want lists. Unlimited reporting capabilities. Maintain multiple collections for as many collections as you need, even if we do not have a price guide yet. Telephone technical support number included in package, printed manual and on-screen help.

Only $49.95
Plus $5.00 Shipping & Handling per guide. Each additional guide only $15.00. Please specify 3.5" floppy or CD.

PRICE GUIDES AVAILABLE FOR:
PRECIOUS MOMENTS® COMPANY DOLLS, Precious Moments Applause® Dolls, Precious Moments® by Enesco, Hallmark Ornaments now including Hallmark Kiddie Car Classics and Hallmark Merry Miniatures, Cherished Teddies®, Boyds Collection, soon Beanie Babies and many more. List available.

Rosie Wells Enterprises, Inc.
22341 E. Wells Rd., Canton, IL 61520
Phone: 800/445-8745 or Fax 309/668-2795

30 day money back guarantee. IBM compatible, 486 or better, 8 MB RAM or better (Mac with SoftWindows).
©1997 Hallmark Cards, Inc., ©1997 Precious Moments, Inc. Licensee Rosie Wells Enterprises, Inc., All Rights Reserved. ©1997 Department 56, Licensee Rosie Wells Enterprises, Inc., Cherished Teddies ©1991-1997 Priscilla Hillman, Licensee Enesco Corporation. Cherished Teddies® is a registered trademark of Enesco Corporation.

Precious Pals

Precious Pals made their debut in September, 1997. Six animals have been chosen from the Precious Moments videos to start the parade of 6" bean-filled animals.

1734	**Georgina – Giraffe**	☐
1735	**Jeremy – Toucan**	☐
1736	**Hopper – Bird**	☐
1737	**Simon – Blue Lamb**	☐
1738	**Dudley – Dog**	☐
1739	**Snowflake – Rabbit**	☐

Comments: Issued September, 1997, 6" Tall.
Secondary Market Value: Current
Purchased From _____ Date _____
Orig. S.R. $6.00   I paid $_____

Gill - Fish ☐

Comments: Issued July, 1997, 6" Tall.
Gill was a special Precious Pal given to the folks that registered for the 1997 Licensee event. He was limited to 1,750 pieces and was completely distributed in less than 36 hours! Only one sale has been reported to Rosie's office of $175, but this is not enough to establish a price.
Secondary Market Value: NE
Purchased From _____ Date _____
Orig. S.R. $6.00   I paid $_____

Songs of the Spirit

1076   Faith – Harp
Comments: Issued 1995, 16" Tall.
Dressed in a pale lavender and blue gown trimmed with white lace, Faith will play her harp and sing the songs she heard David sing in the Book of Psalms.
Secondary Market Value: Current
Purchased From _____ Date _____
Orig. S.R. $50.00   I paid $_____

1077   Love – Violin
Comments: Issued 1995, 16" Tall.
In her vivid, pink taffeta and lace gown, Love will play a message that love is not love until it is given away.
Secondary Market Value: Current
Purchased From _____ Date _____
Orig. S.R. $50.00   I paid $_____

1078   Hope – Trumpet
Comments: Issued 1995, 16" Tall.
In her angelic, pale yellow satin and white lace gown, Hope will play a melody to let everyone know that after one has gone through a storm, it is time to look toward Heaven to see God's rainbow. Hope was first introduced in late 1994 as an exclusive doll of the QVC Shopping Channel, but then later became available to Precious Moments Company retail dealers.
Secondary Market Value: Current
Purchased From _____ Date _____
Orig. S.R. $50.00   I paid $_____

1079   Charity – French Horn
Comments: Issued 1995, 16" Tall.
In her heavenly, blue satin dress, Charity loves to play a joyful tune on her french horn to put a smile on everyone's face and song in the heart.
Secondary Market Value: Current
Purchased From _____ Date _____
Orig. S.R. $50.00   I paid $_____

Sweetheart Series

1029 Rachel
First in Series
Retired – July, 1993

Comments: Issued October, 1991, 16" Tall.
Having the reputation as being the first doll in the series, Rachel was also the first brunette-haired doll for the Precious Moments Company. She has a beautiful hair style, as two side braids are pulled to the back to blend in with her long tresses. Rachel is wearing a lovely red and white gown with tiers of white lace. Wearing a gold heart-shaped locket, she reminds us that love comes from the heart. In 1993, her retail price increased to $45.00.

Secondary Market Value: $200-250
Purchased From _____ Date _____
Orig. S.R. $40.00/$45.00   I paid $_____

1037 Emily
Limited to One Year of Production
Second in Series

Comments: Issued October, 1992, 16" Tall.
In her simplistic, white gown trimmed with pink lace on the sleeves and a pink sash, she appears to be a Valentine princess. Emily has a very delicate headband of blue flowers and a lovely, gold, oval locket necklace. She is holding a pink heart-shaped pillow trimmed with white lace.

Secondary Market Value: $175-200
Purchased From _____ Date _____
Orig. S.R. $50.00   I paid $_____

1053 Amber
Third in Series

Comments: Issued 1994, 16" Tall.
Amber is dressed in a pretty, pink taffeta dress with an overlay of lace on the bodice. Two petite rosettes and a pink heart gather each side of the front hemline of her skirt to give it a scalloped effect and show her white lace petticoat. Even her pink satin headband is adorned with a pink bow bearing another heart and rosette. Being the perfect little lady, she wears lace gloves.

Secondary Market Value: $150-180
Purchased From _____ Date _____
Orig. S.R. $55.00   I paid $_____

Sweetheart Series

1083 Courtney
Limited to One Year of Production
Fourth in Series
Comments: Issued 1995, 16" Tall.
Dressed in a pink and white heart print dress, Courtney is ready to be the symbol of love. Her white yoke collar has delicate beading in the shape of a heart and she wears a satin headband with pink roses.
Secondary Market Value: $110-150
Purchased From _____ Date _____
Orig. S.R. $50.00   I paid $_____

1090 Rosemary
Limited to One Year of Production
Fifth in Series
Comments: Issued 1996, 16" Tall.
She is dressed in a bright red dress with the collar and overskirt done in a floral print, trimmed with eyelet lace. Rosemary has a ribbon rose at her neckline and holds a red rose in her hand.
Secondary Market Value: $80-100
Purchased From _____ Date _____
Orig. S.R. $45.00   I paid $_____

1061 Hannah
Sixth in Series
Comments: Issued 1997, 16" Tall.
Dressed for a formal Valentine party, Hannah's flowing gown is made of white satin. The gown's skirt has a cascade of pink hearts. Hannah has pink, heart-shaped buttons on the bodice and cuffs of her gown.
Secondary Market Value: Current
Purchased From _____ Date _____
Orig. S.R. $50.00   I paid $_____

1119 Chloe
Seventh in Series
Comments: Issued 1997, 16" Tall.
Chloe is dressed in a red satin, ankle length dress which has three tiers of white lace. She wears red satin shoes accented with a gold colored heart.
Secondary Market Value: Current
Purchased From _____ Date _____
Orig. S.R. $50.00   I paid $_____

Wooden Dolls

1218	**Louise**
1219	**Fredrick**

Limited Edition – 1,000

Comments: Issued January, 1996, 12" Tall.
Wooden/Musical Plays: "Edelweiss"
Secondary Market Value for matching numbered set: $1800-2000
Secondary Market Value for unmatched numbered set: $850-950
Secondary Market Value for Louise: $450-500
Secondary Market Value for Fredrick: $400-450
Purchased From_____ Date _____
Orig. S.R. $250.00 ea.   I paid $_____

1231	**Natasha**
1232	**Gertrude**

Limited Edition – 1,000

Comments: Issued January, 1997, 12" Tall.
Wooden/Musical Plays: "God Bless America"
Secondary Market Value for matching numbered: $1000-1200
Secondary Market Value for unmatched numbered: $750-800
Secondary Market Value for single doll: $350-400
Purchased From_____ Date _____
Orig. S.R. $250.00 ea.   I paid $_____

Amway Dolls

1028   Jessica
Limited Edition – 3,000

Comments: Issued 1991, 16" Tall.
She is the very first 16" Precious Moments Company doll ever to be offered as an "Exclusive." She has the same hair style as Patti with Goose but her pink satin ribbons add an elegance to coordinate with her dress. Her old-fashioned dress is made of a dainty pink and tan flowered print. The three tiers of her skirt are trimmed with pink satin ribbon and white lace. She rapidly sold out within two months and very few collectors were even aware of her existence!
Secondary Market Value: $550-600
Purchased From _____ Date _____
Orig. S.R. $49.95   I paid $_____

1033   Melissa
Limited Edition – 4,000

Comments: Issued 1992, 16" Tall.
Melissa is dressed in Christmas colors of red, green and white. Her hair style is the same as the first pink Missy with green bows on top of each pigtail. White lace adds a note of "party time," and she is hoping someone will invite her!
Secondary Market Value: $200-225
Purchased From _____ Date _____
Orig. S.R. $36.99   I paid $_____

1041   Maddy
Limited Edition – 6,000

Comments: Issued 1994, 16" Tall.
Maddy is dressed in a light top and a blue print skirt with a large pink bow accenting her waistline. She wears a big pink bow with blue and pink flowers to make her ready for the holiday parties.
Secondary Market Value: $160-180
Purchased From _____ Date _____
Orig. S.R. $44.99   I paid $_____

Amway

1052 Rebecca
Limited Edition – 5,000
Comments: Issued 1993, 16" Tall.
Rebecca's simple white gown is brought to life with pink iridescent trim on her sleeves, waistline and neckline.
Secondary Market Value: $180-195
Purchased From _____ Date _____
Orig. S.R. $36.99   I paid $_____

1059 Brianna
Limited Edition – 5,500
Comments: Issued 1996, 16" Tall.
She is the sixth exclusive doll produced for Amway. Dressed in satin and bows, the neckline and skirt of Brianna's dress contain a rainbow of colors.
Secondary Market Value: $100-125
Purchased From _____ Date _____
Orig. S.R. $49.95   I paid $_____

1096 Marissa
Limited Edition – 4,500
Comments: Issued 1995, 16" Tall.
Brown eyed Marissa is just waiting for a little girl to take her to a party. Her dress has a pink satin bodice with a pink and white floral skirt. A delicate pink net, trimmed with lace, overlays her skirt. Hot pink ribbons in her hair, around her waist and one at her neckline have been added.
Secondary Market Value: $145-160
Purchased From _____ Date _____
Orig. S.R. $44.99   I paid $_____

1111 Katherine
Limited Edition - 5,000
Comments: Issued 1997, 16" Tall.
Katherine is wearing a long green corduroy skirt with an ivory silk blouse.
Secondary Market Value: Current
Purchased From _____ Date _____
Orig. S.R. $49.95   I paid $_____

Amway, House of Lloyd

1112   **Kiesha**
Limited Edition - 2,500
Comments: Issued 1997, 16" Tall.
Kiesha is dressed exactly like Katherine.
Secondary Market Value: Current
Purchased From _____ Date _____
Orig. S.R. $49.95   I paid $_____

House of Lloyd

Snuggles
Limited Edition – Less than 2,000
Comments: Issued 1992, 16" Tall.
Many secondary market dealers bought Snuggles up quickly and sold them for $65-70 each. In 1994, Precious Moments Company began to produce this bunny with the name Jeremy.
Secondary Market Value: $40
Purchased From _____ Date _____
Orig. S.R. $35.00   I paid $_____

1-900 Collectors' Line©

**Buy - Sell - Trade Collectibles Across the U.S.A.
With "VOICE AD™" on Rosie's collector advertising line!**
Here's how it works! Call 1-900-740-7575

• Listen to Rosie as she directs you to record your own ad or find out what's available for sale!
Press 49 - Precious Moments PMC Dolls

Our 900 number is approved through AT&T! $2.00 per minute.
Touch-tone phone required.
Must be 18 years of age. Any questions? Call us at 309-668-2211.
Voice Ads™ (Since 1991)
by Rosie Wells Enterprises, Inc., 22341 E. Wells Rd., Canton, IL 61520
Collectors' Outreach in Advertising! Buy! Sell! Trade!

Karate Dolls

1499   **Karate Boy**
1498   **Karate Girl**
Comments: Issued 1996, 12" Tall.
Debbie (Butcher) Cho wanted to do something for a very special man in her life, so she designed these dolls for her husband. Bill loves Debbie and he also loves to teach karate, therefore, he loves these special dolls. The girls wear white with red polka dot tops and the boys wear blue and white striped tops under their jackets. The dolls were produced as Caucasian and Asian. A total of 400 dolls were produced.
Secondary Market Value: $60-75 each
Purchased From _____ Date _____
Orig. S.R. $20.00 ea. I paid $_____

LTD Exclusive

1472   **Tonya**
Comments: Issued 1994, 12" Tall.
In her white satin and net dress, she is ready for her first recital. She is wearing pale mint green panties and she has green ribbons accenting her dress and shoes.
Secondary Market Value: $50-60
Purchased From _____ Date _____
Orig. S.R. $19.90   I paid $_____

LTD Exclusive

1473   Little Missy
Comments: Issued 1994, 12" Tall.
This precious little girl is a 12" replica of the first 16" Missy that retired in 1995.
Secondary Market Value: $50-60
Purchased From _____ Date _____
Orig. S.R. $19.90   I paid $_____

1474   Becca
Comments: Issued 1994, 12" Tall.
Becca is dressed for a Christmas party. Her wine-colored satin hat and dress are trimmed with blue satin ribbons and ecru lace.
Secondary Market Value: $50-60
Purchased From _____ Date _____
Orig. S.R. $19.90   I paid $_____

1475   Little Mary
Comments: Issued 1996, 12" Tall.
Dressed in her plaid skirt, forest green corduroy vest and white blouse, Little Mary is ready for her first day of school. There were 7,288 of these dolls produced.
Secondary Market Value: $45-50
Purchased From _____ Date _____
Orig. S.R. $27.90   I paid $_____

1476   Christine
Comments: Issued 1996, 12" Tall.
Ready to go to Grandmother's house, Christine is dressed in a one-piece coatdress. Her underskirt is a very pale lavender and white print, with the dark lavender print overskirt giving the illusion of a coat. Eyelet lace trims her long sleeves and the bottom of her underskirt. There were 4,208 of these dolls produced.
Secondary Market Value: $50-55
Purchased From _____ Date _____
Orig. S.R. $27.90   I paid $_____

LTD Exclusive, Publishers' Clearing House

1477   Candie
Comments: Issued 1996, 12" Tall.
She is dressed in a burgundy floral print skirt, white satin blouse and a black velvet collar that matches her cowboy boots. Candie has pulled the sides of her hair to the top to make a pony tail. She is ready for her first barn dance. There were 8,520 of these dolls produced.
Secondary Market Value: $45-50
Purchased From _____ Date _____
Orig. S.R. $27.90   I paid $_____

Publishers' Clearing House

1441   Cindy
Limited Edition – 10,000
Comments: Issued April, 1996, 12" Tall.
This precious little girl is ready for her first day at kindergarten, as long as she has her security blanket!
Secondary Market Value: Current
Purchased From _____ Date _____
Orig. S.R. $34.95   I paid $_____

The Publications Staff
At Rosie Wells, Ent.

99

QVC

1056   **Nicole**
Limited Edition – 40,000
Comments: Issued 1994, 16" Tall.
Nicole is wearing red flannel pajamas and cap. Her stocking matches the stocking that Nicholas is tucked in. She has beautiful green eyes and her brown hair braids capture everyone's heart. The night before the scheduled Precious Moments show, she captured 40,000 hearts. "Sold Out" flashed across the television screen one hour before the show!
Secondary Market Value: $100-125
Purchased From _____ Date _____
Orig. S.R. $22.71   I paid $_____

Nicholas
Limited Edition – 40,000
Comments: Issued 1993, 16 " Tall.
Known as First Edition Nicholas, he has curlier hair than the Second Edition Nicholas. There were a few other slight differences between the First Edition and Second Edition. (See pg. 23 for Second Edition Nicholas.) Red thread was used to sew on his buttons; a slightly different plaid patch on his stocking and two buttons were sewn on the back.
Secondary Market Value: $150-175
Purchased From _____ Date _____
Orig. S.R. $21.97   I paid $_____

See photos above.

100

QVC

1073   Noel
Limited Edition – 50,000
Comments: Issued 1996, 16" Tall.
Noel, dressed in a Scottish plaid outfit and beret, is ready to be loved by all ages. Her dark brown hair is pulled back to make one beautiful braid. Her stocking is exactly like the '95 stocking having a white patch with holly print and a smaller red plaid patch.
Secondary Market Value: $75-95
Purchased From _____ Date _____
Orig. S.R. $22.71   I paid $_____

1087   Nikki
Limited Edition – 40,000
Comments: Issued 1995, 16" Tall.
Dressed in a winter green outfit and a Christmas red stocking cap, Nikki is ready to put a smile on everyone's face. Her stocking patch has a holly design with white background similar to Noel's.
Secondary Market Value: $85-100
Purchased From _____ Date _____
Orig. S.R. $22.71   I paid $_____

1105   Lindsay
Comments: Issued July, 1996, 16" Tall.
This pretty little tan-haired darling is dressed in a cream colored taffeta and lace dress with yellow, pink and mint green satin ribbons accenting the lower part of her skirt. Lindsay is ready for a garden party or a band concert in the park.
Secondary Market Value: $60-75
Purchased From _____ Date _____
Orig. S.R. $25.95   I paid $_____

QVC

1410   Laurie & Liza
Limited Edition – 9,000

Comments: Issued September, 1996, 12" Tall.
The twins, Laurie (left) and Liza (right) were issued as an "Open Edition." Later in the year, it was announced they would be a "Limited Edition." They were wearing heart print navy blouses and contrasting tan and navy heart print dresses and hats.
Secondary Market Value: $80-95

Purchased From _____ Date _____
Orig. S.R. $31.50   I paid $_____

H26807   Janelle
Limited Edition – 50,000
First in Series

Comments: Issued February, 1997, 12" Tall.
Janelle was introduced as the first doll in the new Pretty As A Princess series. She is holding a garden basket of petite roses and white flowers. Dressed in a pale pink long-sleeved dress, graciously accented by silver trimmed, pink satin ribbon and white lace, she is ready to be invited into everyone's heart.
Secondary Market Value: Current

Purchased From _____ Date _____
Orig. S.R. $17.95   I paid $_____

And let the beauty of the Lord our God be upon us:
and establish thou the work of our hands upon us...
Psalm 90:17

Spiegel Exclusive

2012 **Gloria**
       Limited Edition – Less than 2,000
Comments: Issued 1996, 12" Tall.
This 12" tree topper is a replica of the 16" Classic Gloria produced in 1995.
Secondary Market Value: $50-60
Purchased From _____ Date _____
Orig. S.R. $29.95   I paid $_____

Sports Doll Collection From Hy-Vee

1629	Tina – Tennis	1633	Flint – Football
1630	Gordon – Golf	1634	Cassie – Cheerleader
1631	Benson – Basketball	1635	Sydney – Soccer
1632	Sadie – Softball	1636	Hanford – Hockey

Comments: Issued May, 1997, 14" Tall.
A cloth doll collection which at press time is exclusive only to Hy-Vee Grocery Stores.
Secondary Market Value: Current
Purchased From_____Date _____
Orig. S.R. $25.00   I paid $_____

Cory

By Jan Kropenick

In 1986, Sam Butcher had the honor of being presented to President Corazon Aquino at the Malacanang Palace in Manila. As usual, Sam wanted to do something for this very special precious moment. He designed a 16" Filipino doll with black curly hair wearing a yellow dress with a faint flower print. The yellow represented "freedom." "Cory" is printed on the bodice and she wears homemade glasses in real gold frames. Cory is on display at the Chapel.

Two leaders were selected from each of the following fields: industry, business, medicine and education. One of the two people from each field would be chosen to speak. During Sam's speech, he presented the doll to President Aquino. Experiencing this very special moment, she ordered one hundred dolls so that she could present them as gifts from the Malacanang Palace. There are approximately 25-30 in the United States.

At two different Precious Moments events, one being at Rosie's and Dave's annual convention for PM collectors, Sam hid a doll shoe under one of the seats and then announced to the audience to look for the shoe. Sam then presented a Cory to them. This is known as a "Sam Butcher Cinderella Story!" (See pg. 43 for entry.)

Hi Babies, A Sam Butcher Original

In 1986, 1987 and 1988, Samson Company distributed Hi Babies for the Samuel J. Butcher Company. In 1989, Precious Moments Country, Inc. continued the distribution of these dolls. It would take another guide book to individually identify each doll and the variations of many dolls. Therefore, a bird's eye view will be given and secondary market prices will help in giving guidelines for insurance purposes when selling a collection.

The first dolls only carried a sticker on the bottom of one shoe. "Made in the Philippines for Samuel J. Butcher Company – 1986." This doll is considered a "No Mark" as these stickers readily came off. The following year, the same information was imprinted on the sole of one shoe, but did not carry a date. The word Love is usually represented in the sayings on the doll's clothing by a little heart design.

The above picture shows the Graduate Girl dressed in white with "Class of 87" in pink print. The Boy Graduate is not pictured, but he is dressed in a black gown with "Class of 87" in white print. In 1988, the Graduate Girl is dressed in a white gown with "Class of 88" in red print and the boy is dressed in a grey gown with the same white print. The graduate dolls are rare, as only one doll in fifty of the original general distribution was to be a graduate. Many of the earliest dolls had the "hearts" embroidered on their outfit. Others had the saying embroidered on their garments. These dolls have always commanded a higher value. Also, in the above picture, the boy in the upper right has "XOX" embroidered on his suit. The boy in the center demonstrates one of the many plaid outfits, although his saying, "Smile, God Loves You," is rare. "Happy Birthday" is very rare. This birthday doll happened to have a hair cut from a very special person named Phil Butcher. I'm sure Phil had tears rolling down his face, as he was laughing and cutting away all traces of the doll's curly

Hi Babies

hair. This is only one example of how Phil could put laughter into other people's lives.

The little girl in red has her saying embroidered on her outfit.

All the dolls from the Samson Company had yarn hair, either fine or coarse. Both the girls and the boys had straight or curly hair and the usual hair coloring was yellow, tan or dark brown. Some dolls were made with different hair coloring: pink, peach, aqua, blue and purple. These dolls were very difficult to find.

The little boy in the upper left corner sports blue hair and the little girl to his right has purple hair. The two dolls with black silk hair were exclusive to Rosie's 1990 Precious Moments Convention in Joplin. These two Caucasian dolls are the only ones with black silk hair except for PAL, the Philippines doll seen below. PAL stands for Philippine Air Lines.

The three college kids, University of Nebraska, Penn State and Fighting Irish are just a few of the college dolls that are extremely rare.

The Doctor and Nurse dolls did not stay on the shelves very long, as many collectors happened to be in the medical profession.

"Future Las Vegas Showgirl" came in yellow or peach dresses. She is the only caucasian doll to have black yarn hair, and the only doll to have long hair which is twisted into a fashionable bun in the back and decorated with flowers.

The little girl in the lower right hand corner was given to my daughter, Cindy, by Jim Malcom, who had been Phil Butcher's closest friend. She is a prototype for a Wee Baby, which was never produced.

Dolls distributed by Samson Company
Dolls with pastel hair color - add $20 to given price
Dolls with embroidered ♥ and sayings - add $20 to given price.

106

Clubs:
Unique Flock (Exclusive) $55-60

Colleges: (Exclusive)
Fightin' Irish $90-95
Michigan State $90-95
Ohio State.................................... $90-95
Penn State.................................... $90-95
(TCU) Texas Christian University .. $90-95
University of Florida $90-95
University of Kentucky $90-95
University of Nebraska $90-95
University of Tennessee............... $90-95

Family:
I ♥ Dad $30-35
#1 Dad... $40-45
I ♥ Mom $30-35
I ♥ Grandma $40-45
I ♥ Grandpa $40-45

General:
Beach Boy/Beach Girl $30-35
I ♥ Country $30-35
I ♥ You.. $30-35
I ♥ The Beach.............................. $30-35
Keep On Truckin' $30-35
Jesus Loves Me $45-50
Smile, God Loves You $45-50
You Are My Sunshine.................. $45-50
You're The Greatest..................... $30-35

Graduation: (Boy & Girl)
"87" $45-50
"88" $40-45

Medical: (Nurse & Doctor)
"Get Well Soon".......................... $50-55
"You're The Greatest" $50-55

Special Days:
Be My Valentine (Rare) $55-60
Happy Birthday (Rare) $55-60
It's A Boy..................................... $30-35
It's A Girl $30-35
Happy Mother's Day (Rare)......... $55-60
Merry Christmas.......................... $30-35

California:
I ♥ California $30-35
I ♥ S.F. (San Francisco)................. $30-35
I ♥ San Francisco $30-35
I Left My ♥ in San Francisco $30-35
Best Mom in California................ $30-35
Go Climb A Street (S.F.) $30-35
"Pier 39" (Exclusive).................... $55-60
I ♥ Chinatown (Exclusive)............ $55-60

Colorado:
Estes Park, Colo. (Exclusive) $55-60

Florida:
I ♥ Fla. $30-35
I ♥ Florida $30-35
I ♥ Busch Gardens (Tampa) $55-60

Georgia:
Georgia Peach.............................. $30-35
Best Mom in Georgia $30-35
I ♥ Dahlonega (Old mining town
north of Atlanta, exclusive to
gift shop/fudge factory)..................... $55-60

Kentucky:
I ♥ Kentucky (Cowboy & Cowgirl) .. $30-35

Michigan:
Say "Yes" to Michigan "Holland"
(Dutch boy and girl, exclusive to
gift shop in Holland, Michigan) ... $55-60

Missouri:
I ♥ St. Louis $30-35
Silver Mines (Exclusive to
entertainment park)..................... $55-60

Nevada:
Future Las Vegas Showgirl $35-40
I ♥ Las Vegas $30-35

Oklahoma:
I ♥ Oklahoma (Cowboy & Cowgirl) $30-35

Tennessee:
I ♥ Tennessee (Cowboy & Cowgirl) $30-35

Texas:
Best Mom in Texas...................... $30-35
Texas Star.................................... $30-35

Hi Babies

In 1989, the data would be imprinted on the sole of the shoe which also carried the previous information, "Made in the Philippines for Samuel J. Butcher Company."

In 1990, the dolls would be given silk hair, ranging in colors from blonde, tan and red. Each doll would carry the same heart shaped tag on a little elastic band.

This picture depicts the dolls with silk hair but, for some unknown reason, all these dolls, except for the Chapel Angel, are dressed in outfits from the Samson era.

The Chapel Angel was exclusive to the Chapel Gift Shop. This particular angel is a prototype, as it has "U.S.A." on the gown.

The following dolls were produced from 1990 through 1992. The original price was $12, but dropped to $10 just prior to the dolls being discontinued.

Secondary Market Value $25-$30

General Line:
Daddy's Little Girl
Daddy's Little Boy
Friend at Heart - Girl
Grandma's Little Girl
Grandma's Little Boy
Grandma ♥ Me - Girl
Grandma ♥ Me - Boy
Hallelujah Country - Girl
Hallelujah Country - Boy
Happy 50th - Girl
Happy 50th - Boy
Happy 40th - Girl
Happy 40th - Boy
I ♥ Precious Moments - Girl
I ♥ Precious Moments - Boy
Irish at Heart - Girl
Jesus Loves Me - Girl
Hugs & Kisses - Girl
Mommy's Little Girl
Mommy's Little Boy
Over the Hill - Girl
Over the Hill - Boy

Arizona:
I ♥ Arizona - Girl
I ♥ Arizona - Boy
Grand Canyon, AZ - Girl
Grand Canyon, AZ - Boy
I ♥ the Grand Canyon - Girl
I ♥ the Grand Canyon - Boy

Colorado:
High On Colorado - Girl
High On Colorado - Boy
I ♥ Colorado - Girl
I ♥ Colorado - Boy
Rocky Mountain National Park - Girl
Rocky Mountain National Park - Boy

Florida:
Florida Beach - Girl
Florida Beach - Boy
Florida Sunshine - Girl
Florida Sunshine - Boy
I ♥ Florida - Girl
I ♥ Florida - Boy

Georgia:
Georgia Peach - Girl

Massachusetts:
Boston - Girl
Boston - Boy
I ♥ Boston - Girl
I ♥ Boston - Boy

Michigan:
I ♥ Michigan - Girl
I ♥ Michigan - Boy
Michigan - Girl
Michigan - Boy
Say Yes to Michigan - Girl
Say Yes to Michigan - Boy

Hi Babies

New Jersey:
I ♥ N.J. - Girl
I ♥ N.J. - Boy
I ♥ New Jersey - Girl
I ♥ New Jersey - Boy
New Jersey Perfect Together - Girl
New Jersey Perfect Together - Boy

New Mexico:
Albuquerque - Girl
Albuquerque - Boy
New Mexico - Girl
New Mexico - Boy
NM Land of Enchantment - Girl
NM Land of Enchantment - Boy

New York:
I ♥ NY - Girl
I ♥ NY - Boy
I ♥ New York - Girl
I ♥ New York - Boy
I ♥ Rochester - Girl
I ♥ Rochester - Boy
I ♥ Buffalo - Girl
I ♥ Buffalo - Boy

Texas:
Don't Mess with Texas - Girl
Don't Mess with Texas - Boy

There were several exclusive Hi Babies produced in 1990-1991.

Although Enesco obtained the license to produce Hi Babies, Precious Moments Company retained the license to produce exclusive Hi Babies. The minimum order of one hundred dolls may still be ordered. Further information may be obtained by calling 1-800-248-9738.

The following dolls are exclusive to named stores or companies and were produced by Precious Moments Company.

Arizona:
Made for Lake Havasu City, AZ
"London Bridges, Lake Havasu City, AZ" - Girl
"London Bridges, Lake Havasu City, AZ" - Boy
Orig. price $14 ea., Secondary $60-65

Arkansas:
Passion Play in Eureka Springs, Arkansas
"Jesus Loves You" - Girl dressed in pink
"Jesus Loves You" - Boy dressed in blue
Orig. price $14 ea., Secondary $60-65

Colorado:
"Durdingo" - Boy
Orig. price $14, Secondary $60-65

Georgia:
I ♥ Blairsville - Girl
I ♥ Blairsville - Boy
Orig. price $14 ea., Secondary $60-65

Missouri:
Christy Theatre in Branson, MO
Christy Lane - "One Day at a Time" is on the small circular stage which features a doll dressed in a hot pink dress standing in front of a microphone.
The theatre is no longer in existence.
Orig. price $16, Secondary $90-95
"I Love Joplin - 1990" - Jan's Nest

Rosie Wells' Precious Moments Convention in Joplin
Girl - in pink outfit with black silk hair
Girl - in yellow outfit with black silk hair
Orig. price $12 ea., Secondary $45-50
Carthage, MO True Value Hardware Store
Girl - dressed in mauve outfit
Girl - dressed in peach outfit
Boy - dressed in green outfit
Boy - dressed in blue outfit
Orig. price $14 ea., Secondary $60-65
Precious Moments Chapel Gift Shop
Timmy the Angel - "Precious Moments Chapel - Carthage, Missouri"
Orig. price $14, Secondary $65-70

Tennessee:
"Casey Jones" - Boy in railroad engineer outfit made for the Casey Jones Village - Silverton Railroad in Jackson, TN.
Orig. price $14, Secondary $60-65
"Dollywood" - Dolly Parton Enterprises, Pigeon Forge, TN
Girl dressed in cowgirl outfit
Orig. price $12.95, Secondary $60-65
"I ♥ the Grand Ole Opry" Nashville, TN - Girl
"I ♥ the Grand Ole Opry" Nashville, TN - Boy
Orig. price $12.50 ea,, Secondary $60-65

Hi Bunnies

See Photo Above

1701	**Pink Bunny**	☐
1702	**Mint Green Bunny**	☐
1703	**White Bunny**	☐
1704	**Yellow Bunny**	☐
1705	**Peach Bunny**	☐
1706	**Blue Bunny**	☐

Comments: Issued 1990, 6" Tall. "Some Bunny Loves You"
Secondary Market Value: $20-25
Purchased From _____ Date _____
Orig. S.R. $12.50   I paid $_____

See Photo Above

1710	**Pink Bunny**	☐
1713	**Blue Bunny**	☐
1716	**Peach Bunny**	☐
1719	**White Bunny**	☐

Comments: Issued 1991, 6" Tall. "I Love You"
Secondary Market Value: $20-25
Purchased From _____ Date _____
Orig. S.R. $12.50   I paid $_____

Hi Bunnies

See
Photo
Page 110

1711	**Pink Bunny**	☐
1714	**Blue Bunny**	☐
1717	**Peach Bunny**	☐
1720	**White Bunny**	☐

Comments: Issued 1991, 6" Tall.
"Get Well Soon"
Secondary Market Value: $20-25
Purchased From _____ Date _____
Orig. S.R. $12.50   I paid $_____

See
Photo
Page 110

1712	**Pink Bunny**	☐
1715	**Blue Bunny**	☐
1718	**Peach Bunny**	☐
1721	**White Bunny**	☐

Comments: Issued 1991, 6" Tall.
"Hoppy Birthday"
Secondary Market Value: $20-25
Purchased From _____ Date _____
Orig. S.R. $12.50   I paid $_____

Hi Bunny ☐

Comments: Issued 1991, 6" Tall.
Dealers were given extra bibs the last few weeks of distribution of the bunnies. These bibs are considered rare.
Secondary Market Value: $35-40
Purchased From _____ Date _____
Orig. S.R. $12.50   I paid $_____

1783   **Christmas Hi Baby in Sleigh** ☐
        Limited to One Year of Production – 1993

Comments: Issued 1993, 6" Tall.
In 1993, this happy baby was enjoying her first sleigh ride. Dressed in her red Christmas hooded sleeper, supported by a black and red pillow and wrapped in a blanket, she had her wishes printed on her white wooden sleigh, "Happy Holly-days!"
Secondary Market Value: $50-60
Purchased From _____ Date _____
Orig. S.R. $25.00   I paid $_____

Welcome Home Babies

These three precious babies are wearing either blue, pink or pastel yellow flannel hooded sleepers. They each have a white receiving blanket with colored satin binding to match the sleeper and a satin ribbon saying, "Welcome Home, Baby." They have matching white wooden cradles. Children can play with the doll but the cradle is so fragile, it must be used only as decoration.

1780 **Yellow**
Discontinued – 1994
Comments: Issued 1992, 6" Tall.
Secondary Market Value: $50-60
Purchased From _____ Date _____
Orig. S.R. $25.00   I paid $_____

1781 **Blue**
Discontinued – 1994
Comments: Issued 1992, 6" Tall.
Secondary Market Value: $50-60
Purchased From _____ Date _____
Orig. S.R. $25.00   I paid $_____

1782 **Pink**
Discontinued – 1994
Comments: Issued 1992, 6" Tall.
Secondary Market Value: $60-70
Purchased From _____ Date _____
Orig. S.R. $25.00   I paid $_____

Welcome Home, Baby

Bears, bunnies and all of God's other creatures that might be produced by Precious Moments Company in the future, are made to be hugged and loved. Animals bring the right greeting to anyone and everyone. These cuddly animals are made for both boys and girls from age one to ninety-nine years. Many people don't realize that either Grandpa or Grandma may never have had a teddy bear when they were a child and are delighted when that wish of having their very own comes true.

Over the years, many collectors no longer have the animals in their Precious Moments collection as they have been the "Perfect Gift." Unfortunately, one tends not to replace it immediately. A year goes by and it is not available on the current market, nor can one even find it! Don't forget they are made for hugging. Have you hugged your bear or bunny today? Please remember to remove all tags before giving the animals to small children.

Earlier plush made for Precious Moments® were licensed by Applause®. See our Price Guide for Precious Moments™ Applause® Dolls for more information.

Gimme A Bear Hug

The first bears arrived with the inner part of their ear being white instead of brown. One catalog company happened to have these bears. A few folks have black bears but these were prototypes. Secondary market value for these "black" bears would be $75-80. (See photo below of one errored bear and the prototype black bear.)

1730   **White**
Discontinued – December, 1991
Comments: Issued 1991, 6" Tall.
Secondary Market Value: $25-30
Secondary Market Value Errored Ears: $35-40
Purchased From _____ Date _____
Orig. S.R. $12.50   I paid $_____

Seven Hugs A Day
Keeps Grumpiness Away!

113

Gimme a Bear Hug

1731   **Grey**
              Discontinued – December, 1991
Comments: Issued 1991, 6" Tall.
Secondary Market Value: $25-30
Secondary Market Value Errored Ears: $35-40
Purchased From _____ Date _____
Orig. S.R. $12.50   I paid $_____

1732   **Brown**
              Discontinued – 1992
Comments: Issued 1991, 6" Tall.
This brown bear was produced in 1991 and 1992. The retail price decreased in 1992, to $10.00.
Secondary Market Value: $25-30
Secondary Market Value Errored Ears: $35-40
Purchased From _____ Date _____
Orig. S.R. $12.50   I paid $_____

1740   **Pink Teddy Bear**
              Discontinued – December, 1992
Comments: Issued 1991, 12" Tall.
This adorable pink bear wears its heart on its right paw. The heart reads, "Squeeze Me" and if you do squeeze it you will hear a squeak. Of course, it's the little bear's way of saying, "I Love You, Too!"
Secondary Market Value: $85-100
Purchased From _____ Date _____
Orig. S.R. $32.00   I paid $_____

1741   **Blue Teddy Bear**
              Discontinued – December, 1992
Comments: Issued 1991, 12" Tall.
This adorable blue bear was made to be loved! Teaching baby to "Squeeze Me" starts little hands in simple coordination. Once baby has learned to get teddy's response, remember, "Happy noise" is wonderful!
Secondary Market Value: $85-100
Purchased From _____ Date _____
Orig. S.R. $32.00   I paid $_____

Plush

1725   Simon The Lamb – Blue
Discontinued

Comments: Issued 1995, 6" Tall.
This precious, little blue lamb is God's messenger from the video, "Simon the Lamb." Certainly, Psalms 23:1 reminds us, "The Lord is my Shepherd..." and no matter what color we are, He loves us all, including blue lambs.
Secondary Market Value: $20-25
Purchased From _____ Date _____
Orig. S.R. $10.00   I paid $_____

1726   Simon the Lamb – White
Discontinued

Comments: Issued 1995, 6" Tall.
In the video, Simon was a white lamb before Timmy the Angel accidentally tipped a can of blue paint over, while painting a rainbow in the heavens. The paint fell on Simon, but God knows "it's who you are on the inside that counts."
Secondary Market Value: $30-40
Purchased From _____ Date _____
Orig. S.R. $10.00   I paid $_____

1742   Charlie

Comments: Issued 1993, 15" Tall.
Little Charlie is the perfect gift for the little arms that want to hug him. He is a cute brown bear with a tuft of tan hair on top of his head. His little tail is also tan. Of course, we all know that Charlie has a belly button just like the bigger bears. Original retail decreased as of July, 1997.
Secondary Market Value: Current
Purchased From _____ Date _____
Orig. S.R. $22.50/$15.00   I paid $_____

Plush

1743   Charlie
Comments: Issued 1993, 21" Tall.
This 21" cuddly bear is the ideal gift for the person who may be having chest or heart surgery. He makes a wonderful substitute for a pillow to hold against the chest when one has to cough. Charlie does absorb a lot of discomfort and loves a lot of hugs. He is made for children, but aren't we all God's Children? Original retail decreased as of July, 1997.
Secondary Market Value: Current
Purchased From _____ Date _____
Orig. S.R. $37.50/$25.00   I paid $_____

1744   Charlie
Comments: Issued 1993, 48" Tall.
Charlie is made to be loved and loves putting his arms around little ones while they watch Precious Moments videos. He doesn't even mind having a little one sit on his lap. He really gets out of shape if children play too rough with him. Original retail decreased as of July, 1997.
Secondary Market Value: Current
Purchased From _____ Date _____
Orig. S.R. $300.00/$250.00   I paid $_____

1745   Snowball
Discontinued – January, 1997
Comments: Issued 1993, 15" Tall.
Snowball was first introduced in the Chapel Gift Shop, just in time for the 1993 Christmas events. In February, 1994, he became available to retail dealers. He was a very popular Christmas gift with his own red ribbon. He can only be found on the secondary market.
Secondary Market Value: $45-50
Purchased From _____ Date _____
Orig. S.R. $22.50   I paid $_____

... Suffer the little children to come unto me, and forbid them not: for of such is the kingdom of God.

Mark 10:14

Plush

1746	**Blue Bear**
1747	**Pink Bear**
1748	**Brown Bear**
	Discontinued – May, 1996

Comments: Issued 1994, 9" Tall.
This bear is just the right size for those little hands to hold. This little bear has a matching ribbon tied around its neck saying, "Baby's First." The Brown Bear could be considered a miniature Charlie bear. Introductory price of $8.76 increased to $10.00 in 1995.
Secondary Market Value for Pink and Blue: $25-35
Secondary Market Value for Brown: $20-25
Purchased From _____ Date _____
Orig. S.R. $8.76/$10.00   I paid $_____

See Photo Above

1749   **Bride Bear**

Comments: Issued 1995, 15" Tall.
Although this bear arrived in the early part of 1995, they decided to have a June wedding in time to honeymoon in Carthage, MO, during the first Licensee Show. The Bride, holding her little bouquet of flowers, has flowers adorning the crown of her white veil. She knows that she will be attending many bridal showers and weddings in the future. Original retail decreased as of July, 1997.
Secondary Market Value: Current
Purchased From _____ Date _____
Orig. S.R. $25.00/$20.00   I paid $_____

Plush

1750   Groom Bear
Comments: Issued 1995, 15" Tall.
Although this bear arrived in the early part of 1995, they decided to have a June wedding in time to honeymoon in Carthage, MO, during the first Licensee Show. It is interesting to note that the male attendees at the show were the buyers of the groom. Original retail decreased as of July, 1997.
Secondary Market Value: Current
Purchased From _____ Date _____
Orig. S.R. $25.00/$20.00   I paid $_____

1751   Cupid Bear
Comments: Issued 1995, 15" Tall.
In 1995, the first shipment of cupid bears arrived with a very unhappy look on their faces. Precious Moments Company decided this cupid bear did not depict the "Happiness" of a cupid; therefore, these bears were never released to retail dealers. "Seek and ye shall find," as many collectors have found these bears and they are available on the secondary market.
Secondary Market Value: $40-60
Purchased From _____ Date _____
Orig. S.R. $25.00   I paid $_____

1757   Snowball with Vest
         Discontinued – January, 1997
Comments: Issued July, 1995, 15" Tall.
Snowball decided he wanted to dress up for the coming Christmas season. He sports a red, satin bow around his neck and wears a handsome plaid vest.
Secondary Market Value: Current
Purchased From _____ Date _____
Orig. S.R. $25.00   I paid $_____

Plush

1758 Bailey Bunny
Comments: Issued 1996, 15" Tall.
Bailey arrived just before Easter 1996. All grandmothers need one or two extra Bailey Bunnies just in case the grandchildren visit and announce, "Nana, I didn't get a bunny." Original retail decreased as of July, 1997.
Secondary Market Value: Current
Purchased From _____ Date _____
Orig. S.R. $22.50/$20.00   I paid $_____

1763 Landon
Comments: Issued January, 1997, 15" Tall.
He is the second bear to sport the tannish grey with white-tipped fur. (Grant was the first.) Landon is very proud of his plaid bow and looks like he would giggle because his embroidered Precious Moments patch is tickling his foot. Original retail decreased as of July, 1997.
Secondary Market Value: Current
Purchased From _____ Date _____
Orig. S.R. $25.00/$20.00   I paid $_____

1764 Letty
Comments: Issued January, 1997, 15" Tall.
This bear is dressed appropriately to either visit Grandma's house or stay at home with a little girl who will give her lots of love. Of course, red is Letty's favorite color and she just loves her red skirt and matching bow. Original retail decreased as of July, 1997.
Secondary Market Value: Current
Purchased From _____ Date _____
Orig. S.R. $25.00/$20.00   I paid $_____

1765 Edmond
Comments: Issued January, 1997, 15" Tall.
Edmond is the first tan bear. He sports a green, plaid vest and bow. Original retail decreased as of July, 1997.
Secondary Market Value: Current
Purchased From _____ Date _____
Orig. S.R. $25.00/$20.00   I paid $_____

119

Plush

1766   Eyvette
Comments: Issued January, 1997, 15" Tall.
Eyvette could very easily be Edmond's twin sister, as she is also tan. She wears a black skirt and matching bow on her head. Original retail decreased in July, 1997.
Secondary Market Value: Current
Purchased From _____ Date _____
Orig. S.R. $25.00/$20.00   I paid $_____

1767   Trevor
Comments: Issued September, 1997, 21" Tall.
Trevor has grey with white tip plush fur. He is wearing a red Christmas sweater and white scarf.
Secondary Market Value: Current
Purchased From _____ Date _____
Orig. S.R. $30   I paid $_____

1768   Baxter
Comments: Issued September, 1997, 21" Tall.
Baxter has tan with white tip plush fur. He is dressed in a blue sweater with white scarf.
Secondary Market Value: Current
Purchased From _____ Date _____
Orig. S.R. $30   I paid $_____

1769   Grant Bear in Stocking
Comments: Issued December 1996, 15" Tall.
Grant Bear arrived just before Christmas, 1996, and didn't have time for a photo session. He is the first bear to sport the tan fur with the tips of the nap being almost white. He comes out of his stocking for hugs and bedtime snuggling from any little boy or girl.
Secondary Market Value: Current
Purchased From _____ Date _____
Orig. S.R. $25.00   I paid $_____

Christmas Bears Like To Hide In Christmas Trees!

Plush, Patchwork Bears

1770   **Chris Bear in Stocking**
Comments: Issued November, 1996, 11" Tall.
Chris thought it was more important to be under a Christmas tree than to have his picture taken. He comes out of his stocking for all the little ones who want to give him hugs and kisses.
Secondary Market Value: Current
Purchased From _____ Date _____
Orig. S.R. $20.00   I paid $_____

Patchwork Bears

In November, 1996, these three adorable bears swept collectors off their feet, as they were not the traditional pastel colors nor the standard brown. Instantly, they took many collectors down memory lane to the time when toys were made out of scraps of material and sewn by loving hands. They were sold out of the shipping boxes at the Chapel Christmas Event, as the demand was so great there were not enough bears. Of course, many bears were tickled when artist Sam Butcher signed on the bottom of one of their feet.

1760   **Parker Plaid**
Comments: Issued November, 1996, 12" Tall.
Original retail decreased as of July, 1997.
Secondary Market Value: Current
Purchased From _____ Date _____
Orig. S.R. $21.00/$20.00   I paid $_____

1761   **Dillon Denim**
Comments: Issued November, 1996, 12" Tall.
Original retail decreased as of July, 1997.
Secondary Market Value: Current
Purchased From _____ Date _____
Orig. S.R. $21.00/$20.00   I paid $_____

1762   **Colton Corduroy**
Comments: Issued November, 1996, 12" Tall.
Original retail decreased as of July, 1997.
Secondary Market Value: Current
Purchased From _____ Date _____
Orig. S.R. $22.00/$21.00   I paid $_____

History of the Doll Tags

By Jan Kropenick

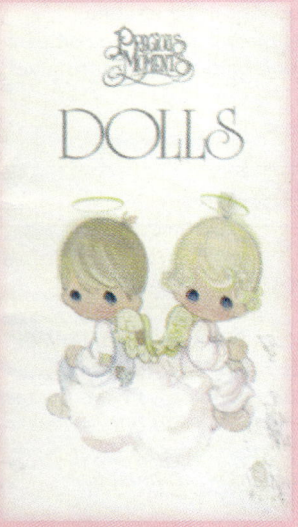

Jonathan & David Company only produced nine 16" dolls. The front of the $1^{3}/_{4}$" x $3^{1}/_{4}$" white tag depicts two angels on a cloud, "But Love Goes On Forever." Inside the tag, one will find the doll's name with a special message to the collector. *"Deep in the heart of the Philippines, young Bible school students spend part of their day producing these 'Happiness In The Lord' dolls. Without this financial assistance they would not be able to complete their education and go into their desired ministries. The Jonathan & David Company of the Philippines began in 1987 when Bill Biel and Sam Butcher became acquainted with a small Bible college in the city of Iloilo, located on the Panay Island. They discovered 33 students were dropping out of the school due to the lack of sufficient funds. It was then that these two men decided to start a company for the sole purpose of supporting these students. These warm and beautiful dolls are the fruit of their labor. Carefully designed and produced with so much love, they are sure to win their way into the hearts of children everywhere."* None of these dolls had a date printed on them.

Samson Company produced the first *Hi Babies*. They did not have tags to identify the very first dolls; one must look at the bottom of their shoes. One shoe carried a sticker label stating it was "Made in the Philippines for the Samuel J. Butcher Company 1986" but these labels came off quite easily. One could say that these dolls had "No Marks." Later, the dolls were produced with an imprint on one shoe stating the same information that the sticker label carried.

In 1989, Precious Moments Country, Inc. changed all white tags to measure $2^{5}/_{8}$" x $3^{1}/_{4}$". The Blue Missy and Pink Missy had a picture of a Precious Moments girl holding a bouquet of flowers with "Missy" on the front of it. She carried the same message on the inside as the Jonathan & David doll tags.

The bride doll Jessi, which was introduced in 1989, had a picture of a bride and Jessi on the front of the tag.

Jonathan & David Company Tag

"Missy" Tag

"Patti with Goose" Tag

Patti with Goose doll could claim she had her own tag, as the $2^{7}/_{8}$" x $2^{3}/_{4}$" white tag had the girl with a goose on the front of it, but with no name. She had to share this tag with the remaining 16" dolls that were produced. The message inside of the tag is as follows: "It is without question that Asia's finest servers are found in the Philippine Islands."

"When Mr. Samuel Butcher visited the Philippines for the first time, he was greatly impressed by the skill of Hongos in the region of Panay. As a result, he established a factory that offered work for needy students and provided Precious Moments dolls for the States. However, because of a growing demand for the dolls, he later transferred to Manila to better accommodate the orders. Now, to continue with his desire to provide education to the needy, much of the Precious Moments Dolls' revenue is used to provide scholarships and vocational opportunities for students throughout the country."

Ozark Annie and Ozark Andy were introduced without tags, but shortly thereafter they were given miniature doll catalog tags. (The first Ozark Annie can readily be identified by her pigtails.)

Jenny and Jordan first had the Goose Girl tag and later, before retiring, had the miniature catalog tag.

In 1989, Precious Moments Country, Inc. introduced the 9" dolls for the on-going series, *Children of the World*. They were first introduced without tags, but in 1991 they were given miniature catalog *Children of the World* tags. In 1993, they were given individual satchel tags with their own names on them.

Miniature Catalog Tag

Children of the World

In 1990, the *Hi Babies* were given little heart tags that were hung around their necks. The earliest dolls had the word "Love" or a heart on the front of their garment.

In 1992, the dolls began to carry the year they were produced. This helps identify *Children of the World* dolls that have been in production over the past five years. The date is imprinted on the doll's back, neck or hair line. Prior to this time, it read, "Made in the Philippines, Precious Moments, Samuel Butcher Co. USA."

In 1993, all dolls began to have their very own individual tags. Many times the doll tag will give you additional information concerning the doll. For instance, one might wonder why Casey, the Precious Moments baseball player, is not dressed in the usual burgundy and white Precious Moments Chapel colors. Casey was born on July 4th and he is wearing the appropriate colors for that day. The Jessi and Baby Lisa tag is unique as it carries Baby Lisa's birth certificate on the inside. Phil has a beautiful certificate that can be framed for display. The Janet and Baby Sarah tag tells everyone of a very special lady.

The *Native American* doll collection tag is also a certificate which is found on the inside of the tag. At the bottom of this certificate the doll's number in the line of production is given. The first series was sold in lots of three sets of matching numbers. The wise person bought a matching set, which has greater value than an unmatched set. The second set of dolls were not sold in this manner.

The Lindsay and Dustin doll tags carry the picture of the real children. One can be sure that Mother Sarah is delighted to share a picture of her "Precious Jewel," and Mother Terri is also bubbling over as she shares a picture of "her pride and joy."

The Garden of Friends series has given each young lady a "watering can" tag, stating first or second edition. The tag gives the month, doll's name and the saying, "Where friendship blooms forever."

The *Jewel Doll* series tag features a foil stamp to match the color of the jewel. Inside the tag is Sam's Biblical interpretation of the gem.

The following animals do not have the stitched "Precious Moments" tags: Simon the Lamb, Bride Bear, Groom Bear and Cupid Bear. Bailey Bunny has a very pretty, pink satin patch with brighter pink stitching on his right foot. Parker Plaid Bear, Colton Corduroy Bear and Dillon Denim Bear have the logos stitched in black on their right foot pad. Charlie Bear (48") has a large burgundy patch, stitched in gold. One must turn him over to see it, as he is almost sitting on it. The two Snowball bears have a bright red oval patch with gold stitching on their lower backs. The remaining bears have the burgundy patch stitched in gold on their right feet.

The following animals wear a white oval plastic tag embossed in gold: (15" and 21") Charlie Bear, Letty Bear, Landon Bear, Edmond Bear, Eyvette Bear, Grant Bear in stocking, Chris Bear in stocking, and Bailey Bunny. There are seven animals in current production that wear white oval paper tags: (48") Charlie, Bride Bear, Groom Bear, Snowball Bear with vest, Parker Plaid Bear, Dillon Denim Bear, and Colton Corduroy Bear.

Note: Please remember to remove all tags prior to giving dolls or animals to any child under three years of age.

Suspension List

1023	Bethany .18	1015	Girl Clown 16
1018	Boy Clown 17	1604	Jonny 34
1067	Brown Baby 24	1026	Kerri 19
2002	Carrie 54	1048	Milly & Her New Baby Doll 22
1022	Casey 18	1031	Sandy .20
1024	Colin 19	2005	Timmy .54
1057	Dawn and Rag Doll 23	1017	Timmy the Angel 16
1043	Dusty 21	1017a	Timmy the Angel blue w/blanket .17
1068	Evie 25	1066	White Baby 24

Retirement List

D008	Blue Missy 3	1506	Misu- Japan 44
1501	Carla - America 42	1010	Ozark Andy 13
2004	Carrie 54	1009	Ozark Annie 13
2003	Christie .54	1002	Patti with Goose 11
1504	Cory - Philippines 43	D009	Patti with Goose 3
1511	Ivan - Russia 46	1035	Phillip .20
1012	Jenny 15	D007	Pink Missy 3
D001	Jesus Loves Me 1	1020	Princess Sincere 17
D002	Jesus Loves Me 1	D003	Private Jo Jo 1
1011	Jonny -16" 14	1029	Rachel .91
1011	Jonny - 17" 14	D004	Sailor Sam 2
1013	Jordan .15	1505	Shonnie - American Indian 43
1025	Katie 19	1510	Sulu - Alaska 46
1502	Mazie - America 42	D006	Taffy 2
1003b	Missy 12	1014	Tiffany .16
1004	Missy 12	D005	Toto 2

Limited Editions

★ Denotes sold out from manufacturer

1067	African-American Baby 24	1065	Erich. . . . . ★ . . . 57
1226	Amber. 86	1219	Fredrick . . . . ★ . . . 93
1053	Amber . . . . ★ . . 91	1232	Gertrude. . . . . ★ . . . 93
1034	Amy. . . . . ★ . . 35		Gill - Fish . . . . ★ . . . 89
1202	Andreah . . . . ★ . . 58	1217	Gloria . . . . ★ . . . 53
2011	Angelica. . . . . ★ . . 56	2012	Gloria - Spiegel Exclusive. . . ★ . . 103
1224	Beryl 85	1100	Gracie. . . . . ★ . . . 27
	Blond Casey . . . . ★ . . . 9	1214	Happy . . . . ★ . . . 59
1462	Blossom - August . . . . ★ . . 63	1466	Holly - December . . . . ★ . . . 65
1059	Brianna. . . . . ★ . . 95	1483	Hopi Maiden. . . . . ★ . . . 76
1210	Bridget . . . . ★ . . 58	1459	Iris - May . . . . ★ . . . 62
1045	Cara . . . . ★ . . 36	1485	Iroquois . . . . ★ . . . 77
1088	Carissa and Baby Tess 76	1403	Jacarila Apache . . . . ★ . . . 79
2015	Celeste. 56	1222	Jade 84
1058	Chapel Indian Doll. . . . . ★ . . . 5	26807	Janelle 102
1401	Chippewa. 78	1030	Janet and Baby Sarah . . . . . ★ . . . 74
1119	Chloe 92	1215	Janna 52
1465	Chrissy - November. . . . . . . ★ . . 64	1455	Jasmine - January. . . . . ★ . . . 61
1783	Christmas Hi Baby . . . . ★ . 111	1230	Jasper. 88
1441	Cindy. 99	1044	Jessi and Baby Lisa . . . . ★ . . . 74
1027	Coleenia . . . . ★ . . . 4	1028	Jessica . . . . ★ . . . 94
1083	Courtney. 92	1111	Katherine 95
1228	Crystal . . . . ★ . . 87	1060	Kathy and Donnie . . . . ★ . . . 75
1458	Daisy - April . . . . ★ . . 62	1036	Katlyn. . . . . ★ . . . 36
1221	Desert Rose 83	1112	Kiesha 96
1103	Dustin 7	1106	Lacey. 37
1947	Dustin 8	1410	Laurie & Liza . . . . ★ . . 102
1037	Emily . . . . ★ . . 91	1457	Lily - March . . . . ★ . . . 61
1064	Emma. . . . . ★ . . 57	1102	Lindsay. 7

125

Limited Editions

1946	Lindsay............................8	1020	Princess Sincere ....★...17
1051	Little Sunshine 36	1518	Pualani......................★...49
1082	Lori and Ginnie...........★...75	1464	Pumpkin - October ....★...64
1218	Louise ....★...93	1052	Rebecca ....★...95
1041	Maddy ....★...94	1081	Robin 37
1606	Maggie....................★...38	1460	Rose - June................★...62
1207	Marcy.....................★...52	1090	Rosemary ....★...92
1096	Marissa...................★...95	1225	Ruby......................★...85
1201	Melinda...................★...58	1227	Sapphire......................86
1033	Melissa...................★...94	1445	Sara and Kara 37
1213	Miakoda..................★...59	1487	Seminole ....★...78
1021	Morning Star 18	1402	Shoshoni 79
1231	Natasha ....★...93	1486	Sioux ....★...77
1404	Navajo 79		Snuggles..................★...96
1063	Nicholas 23	1220	Star 53
	Nicholas ....★..100	1211	Stephanie ....★...52
1056	Nicole....................★..100	1463	Sunny - September ....★...64
1087	Nikki.....................★..101	1605	Sunshine..................★...38
	Nina..........................10	1101	Susan with Twins..........★...75
1073	Noel......................★..101	1607	Valerie ....★...39
1229	Opal..........................87	1115	Victoria......................81
1461	Pansy - July..............★...63	1456	Violet - February ....★...61
1223	Pearl.........................84	1484	Yakima ....★...77
1200	Princess Melody ....★...57	1482	Zuni ....★...76

Sold Out Editions

	4th of July.....................9	1003a	Missy 11
1474	Becca 98	1717	Peach Bunny - Get Well Soon....111
1714	Blue Bunny - Get Well Soon 111	1718	Peach Bunny - Hoppy Birthday...111
1715	Blue Bunny - Hoppy Birthday....111	1716	Peach Bunny - I Love You........110
1713	Blue Bunny - I Love You........110	1705	Peach Bunny
1706	Blue Bunny		Some Bunny Loves You 110
	Some Bunny Loves You 110	1711	Pink Bunny - Get Well Soon 111
1477	Candie 99	1712	Pink Bunny - Hoppy Birthday 111
1476	Christine 98	1710	Pink Bunny - I Love You........110
1751	Cupid Bear 118	1701	Pink Bunny
2006	Harmony......................55		Some Bunny Loves You 110
	Hi Bunny.....................111	1472	Tonya 97
9001	Jamie 8	1720	White Bunny - Get Well Soon....111
1499	Karate Boy 97	1721	White Bunny - Hoppy Birthday...111
1498	Karate Girl....................97	1719	White Bunny - I Love You.......110
1105	Lindsay......................101	1703	White Bunny
1475	Little Mary 98		Some Bunny Loves You 110
1473	Little Missy 98	1704	Yellow Bunny
1702	Mint Green Bunny		Some Bunny Loves You 110
	Some Bunny Loves You 110		

Discontinued

1612	Blue and Yellow Plaid Rag Doll 82	1747	Pink Bear 9" 117
1741	Blue Bear 114	1740	Pink Teddy Bear 12" 114
1746	Blue Bear 9" 117	1611	Red and Blue Plaid Rag Doll 81
1748	Brown Bear 9" 117	1613	Royal Blue Plaid Rag Doll 82
1732	Brown Teddy Bear 12" 114	1725	Simon the Lamb - Blue 115
2002	Carrie - Tree Topper 54	1726	Simon the Lamb - White 115
2004	Carrie - Ornament 54	1745	Snowball Bear 116
2003	Christie - Ornament 54	1757	Snowball w/vest 118
1610	Green and Pink Plaid Rag Doll 81	2005	Timmy 54
1731	Grey Bear 6" 114	1781	Welcome Home Babies - Blue ...112
2006	Harmony......................55	1782	Welcome Home Babies - Pink ...112
1702	Mint Green Bunny	1780	Welcome Home Babies - Yellow .112
	Some Bunny Loves You........110	1730	White Bear 113
2007	Peace - Tree Topper 55		

Alphabetical Listing by Subject

African-American
- ☐ 1117 African-American Baby 29
- ☐ 1067 African-American Baby 24
- ☐ 2001 Carrie 54
- ☐ 1112 Kiesha 96
- ☐ 1062 Viola 23

American Indian
- ☐ 1058 Chapel Indian Doll 5
- ☐ 1401 Chippewa 78
- ☐ 1221 Desert Rose 83
- ☐ 1483 Hopi Maiden 76
- ☐ 1485 Iroquois 77
- ☐ 1403 Jacarila Apache 79
- ☐ 1213 Miakoda 59
- ☐ 1517 Morning Glory - American Indian 49
- ☐ 1021 Morning Star 18
- ☐ 1404 Navajo 79
- ☐ 1020 Princess Sincere 17
- ☐ 1487 Seminole 78
- ☐ 1505 Shonnie - American Indian 43
- ☐ 1402 Shoshoni 79
- ☐ 1486 Sioux 77
- ☐ 1484 Yakima 77
- ☐ 1482 Zuni 76

Angels
- ☐ 2015 Celeste 56
- ☐ 1079 Charity - French Horn 90
- ☐ 1076 Faith - Harp 90
- ☐ 1217 Gloria 53
- ☐ 2009 Gold - Angel 55
- ☐ 1078 Hope - Trumpet 90
- ☐ 2008 Joy 55
- ☐ 1077 Love - Violin 90
- ☐ 2007 Peace 55
- ☐ 1035 Philip 20
- ☐ 2010 Silver 56
- ☐ 1412 Guardian Angel 29
- ☐ 1017 Timmy the Angel 16
- ☐ 1017a Timmy the Angel-blue w/blanket ..17

Baby
- ☐ 1117 African-American Baby 29
- ☐ 1067 African-American Baby 24
- ☐ 1067 Brown Baby 24
- ☐ 1108 Caucasian Baby 28
- ☐ 1109 Hispanic Baby 28
- ☐ 1781 Welcome Home Babies - Blue ...112
- ☐ 1782 Welcome Home Babies - Pink ...112
- ☐ 1780 Welcome Home Babies - Yellow ..112
- ☐ 1066 White Baby 24

Ballerina
- ☐ 1107 Piper 28
- ☐ 1472 Tonya 97

Baseball
- ☐   Casey -Blond 9
- ☐ 1022 Casey 18
- ☐ 1047 Tracey 22

Boy
- ☐ 1408 Air Force Boy 73
- ☐ 1406 Army Boy 72
- ☐ 1631 Benson - Basketball 103
- ☐   Blond Casey 9
- ☐ 1422 Blond Groom 29
- ☐ 1444 Boy in Fatigues 74
- ☐ 1022 Casey 18
- ☐ 1467 Clifford 30
- ☐ 1024 Colin 19
- ☐ 1055 Daniel 5
- ☐ 1103 Dustin 7
- ☐ 1947 Dustin 8
- ☐ 1043 Dusty 21
- ☐ 1065 Erich 57
- ☐ 1633 Flint - Football 103
- ☐ 1219 Fredrick 93
- ☐ 1630 Gordon - Golf 103
- ☐ 1118 Grandpa Bill 29
- ☐ 1493 Groom 31
- ☐ 1636 Hanford - Hockey 103
- ☐ 1515 Hans (Ollie) - Austria 48
- ☐ 1214 Happy 59
- ☐ 1552 Ian 32
- ☐ 1511 Ivan - Russia 46
- ☐ 1722 Jeremy 33
- ☐ D002 Jesus Loves Me 1
- ☐ 1011 Jonny brown tuxedo 14
- ☐ 1011 Jonny dark grey tuxedo 14
- ☐ 1011 Jonny black tuxedo 14
- ☐ 1604 Jonny 34
- ☐ 1013 Jordan 15
- ☐ 1709 Josh 33
- ☐ 1499 Karate Boy 97
- ☐ 1423 Navy Boy 73
- ☐ 1063 Nicholas 23
- ☐ 1010 Ozark Andy 13
- ☐ 1602 Ozark Andy 34
- ☐ 1035 Philip 20
- ☐ D003 Private Jo Jo 1
- ☐ D004 Sailor Sam 2
- ☐   Snuggles 96
- ☐ 1017 Timmy the Angel 16
- ☐ 1017a Timmy the Angel blue w/blanket ..17
- ☐ D005 Toto 2
- ☐ 1499 Young Ho 31

Bride
- ☐ 1421 Blonde Bride 29
- ☐ 1492 Bride 31
- ☐ 1001 Jessi 11
- ☐ 1603 Jessie 34

Christmas
- ☐ 2011 Angelica - Tree Topper 56
- ☐ 1474 Becca 98
- ☐ 2002 Carrie - Tree Topper 54
- ☐ 2004 Carrie - Ornament 54
- ☐ 2015 Celeste - Tree Topper 56
- ☐ 1770 Chris Bear in Stocking 121
- ☐ 2003 Christie - Ornament 54
- ☐ 1783 Christmas Hi Baby in Sleigh 111

127

Alphabetical Listing by Subject

☐	2001	Christy - Tree Topper 53				
☐	1103	Dustin 7				
☐	1947	Dustin 8				
☐	1068	Evie 25				
☐	1217	Gloria 53				
☐	2012	Gloria - Spiegel Exclusive 103				
☐	2009	Gold - Angel Decoration 55				
☐	1769	Grant Bear in Stocking 120				
☐	2006	Harmony - Tree Topper 55				
☐	1552	Ian 32				
☐	1215	Janna 52				
☐	2008	Joy - Tree Topper 55				
☐	1102	Lindsay 7				
☐	1946	Lindsay 8				
☐	1080	Little Mistletoe 25				
☐	1207	Marcy 52				
☐	1551	Natalie 32				
☐	1063	Nicholas 23				
☐		Nicholas 100				
☐	1056	Nicole 100				
☐	1087	Nikki 101				
☐	1073	Noel 101				
☐	2007	Peace - Tree Topper 55				
☐	1550	Regina 32				
☐	2010	Silver - Angel Decoration 56				
☐	1220	Star 53				
☐	1211	Stephanie .52				
☐	2005	Timmy - Tree Topper 54				

Easter

☐	1467	Clifford 30
☐	1468	Winnie 30

First Communion

☐	1490	Christina 30
☐	1491	Grace 31

Girl

☐		4th of July 9
☐	1411	Air Force Girl 73
☐	1524	Aisha - Africa 50
☐	1529	Allison - USA 51
☐	1527	Alohaloni .51
☐	1226	Amber 86
☐	1053	Amber 91
☐	1034	Amy 35
☐	1202	Andreah 58
☐	1439	Angela 30
☐	1514	Angelina - Italy 48
☐	1954	April's Child 41
☐	1405	Army Girl .72
☐	1071	Ashley - Fall 60
☐	1958	August's Child 41
☐	1474	Becca 98
☐	1224	Beryl 85
☐	1075	Bess w/map 6
☐	1023	Bethany - Hispanic 18
☐	1421	Blonde Bride 29
☐	1462	Blossom - August 63
☐	1432	Blossom - August 67
☐	1612	Blue and Yellow Plaid 82
☐	D008	Blue Missy .3
☐	1627	Blueberry .40
☐	1628	Boysenberry 40
☐	1059	Brianna 95
☐	1492	Bride 31
☐	1210	Bridget 58
☐	1069	Brooke - Spring 59
☐	1477	Candie 99
☐	1045	Cara 36
☐	1088	Carissa and Baby Tess 76
☐	1501	Carla - America 42
☐	2002	Carrie 54
☐	2004	Carrie 54
☐	1634	Cassie - Cheerleader 103
☐	1039	Chapel Fan Doll 4
☐	1040	Chapel Fan Doll 5
☐	1058	Chapel Indian Doll 5
☐	1079	Charity - French Horn 90
☐	1401	Chippewa 78
☐	1119	Chloe 92
☐	1465	Chrissy - November 64
☐	1435	Chrissy - November 68
☐	2003	Christie 54
☐	1490	Christina 30
☐	1476	Christine 98
☐	1783	Christmas Hi Baby in Sleigh 111
☐	2001	Christy 53
☐	1441	Cindy 99
☐	1027	Coleenia 4
☐	1097	Colette 7
☐	1089	Colleen 26
☐	1504	Cory - Phillippines 43
☐	1083	Courtney .92

Cloth Dolls

☐	1954	April's Child 41
☐	1958	August's Child 41
☐	1631	Benson - Basketball 103
☐	1612	Blue and Yellow Plaid 82
☐	1627	Blueberry .40
☐	1628	Boysenberry 40
☐	1634	Cassie - Cheerleader 103
☐	1962	December's Child 41
☐	1952	February's Child 41
☐	1633	Flint - Football 103
☐	1630	Gordon - Golf 103
☐	1610	Green and Pink Plaid 81
☐	1636	Hanford - Hockey 103
☐	1951	January's Child 41
☐	1957	July's Child 41
☐	1956	June's Child 41
☐	1953	March's Child 41
☐	1955	May's Child 41
☐	1961	November's Child 41
☐	1960	October's Child 41
☐	1626	Raspberry 40
☐	1611	Red and Blue Plaid 81
☐	1613	Royal Blue Plaid 82
☐	1632	Sadie - Softball 103
☐	1959	September's Child 41
☐	1625	Strawberry 40
☐	1635	Sydney - Soccer 103
☐	1629	Tina - Tennis 103

Clown

☐	1018	Boy Clown 17
☐	1015	Girl Clown 16
☐	1214	Happy 59
☐	D006	Taffy 2
☐	D005	Toto 2

Alphabetical Listing by Subject

☐	1228	Crystal 87	☐	1106	Lacey 37
☐	1458	Daisy - April 62	☐	1410	Laurie & Liza 102
☐	1428	Daisy - April 66	☐	1457	Lily - March 61
☐	1392	Daisy - May 69	☐	1391	Lily - April 69
☐	1057	Dawn and Rag Doll 23	☐	1427	Lily - March 66
☐	1962	December's Child 41	☐	1102	Lindsay 7
☐	1046	Delaney 21	☐	1946	Lindsay 8
☐	1221	Desert Rose 83	☐	1105	Lindsay 101
☐	1086	Ellie 26	☐	1475	Little Mary 98
☐	1037	Emily 91	☐	1473	Little Missy 98
☐	1064	Emma 57	☐	1051	Little Sunshine 36
☐	1068	Evie 25	☐	1082	Lori and Ginnie 75
☐	1076	Faith - Harp 90	☐	1218	Louise 93
☐	1952	February's Child 40	☐	1077	Love - Violin 90
☐	1519	Freya - Denmark 49	☐	1041	Maddy 94
☐	1232	Gertrude 93	☐	1606	Maggie 38
☐	1443	Girl in Fatigues 73	☐	1953	March's Child 41
☐	1217	Gloria 53	☐	1207	Marcy 52
☐	1491	Grace 31	☐	1094	Margaret 27
☐	1100	Gracie 27	☐	1507	Maria - Spain 44
☐	1554	Graduate 32	☐	1398	Marigold - November 71
☐	1104	Gramma's Sweetie 27	☐	1096	Marissa 95
☐	1085	Grandma Martha 26	☐	1084	Maureen 6
☐	1610	Green and Pink Plaid 81	☐	1955	May's Child 41
☐	1512	Gretchen - Germany 47	☐	1502	Mazie - America 42
☐	1508	Gretel - Sweden 45	☐	1070	Megan - Summer 60
☐	1412	Guardian Angel 29	☐	1525	Mei-Mei - China 50
☐	1061	Hannah 92	☐	1201	Melinda 58
☐	1708	Heather 33	☐	1033	Melissa 94
☐	1466	Holly - December 65	☐	1213	Miakoda 59
☐	1436	Holly - December 68	☐	1048	Milly and Her New Baby Doll 22
☐	1399	Holly - December 71	☐	1003a	Missy 11
☐	1078	Hope - Trumpet 90	☐	1003	Missy - Pink 12
☐	1483	Hopi Maiden 76	☐	1092	Missy 12
☐	1459	Iris - May 62	☐	1004	Missy - Blue 12
☐	1429	Iris - May 66	☐	1506	Misu- Japan 44
☐	1485	Iroquois 77	☐	1517	Morning Glory - American Indian 49
☐	1403	Jacarila Apache 79	☐	1390	Morning Glory - March 69
☐	1038	Jackie Ann 21	☐	1021	Morning Star 18
☐	1222	Jade 84	☐	1551	Natalie 32
☐	9001	Jamie 8	☐	1231	Natasha 93
☐	H26807	Janelle 102	☐	1555	Nativity Set 80
☐	1030	Janet and Baby Sarah 74	☐	1404	Navajo 79
☐	1215	Janna 52	☐	1409	Navy Girl 72
☐	1951	January's Child 41	☐	1056	Nicole 100
☐	1455	Jasmine - January 61	☐		Nina 10
☐	1425	Jasmine - January 65	☐	1073	Noel 101
☐	1388	Jasmine - January 68	☐	1087	Nikki 101
☐	1230	Jasper 88	☐	1961	November's Child 41
☐	1012	Jenny 15	☐	1960	October's Child 41
☐	1001	Jessi 11	☐	1523	Ollie - Norway 49
☐	1044	Jessi and Baby Lisa 74	☐	1229	Opal 87
☐	1028	Jessica 94	☐	1009	Ozark Annie 13
☐	1603	Jessi 34	☐	1601	Ozark Annie 34
☐	D001	Jesus Loves Me 1	☐	1461	Pansy - July 63
☐	1957	July's Child 41	☐	1431	Pansy - July 67
☐	1956	June's Child 41	☐	1394	Pansy - July 70
☐	1498	Karate Girl 97	☐	1114	Pat 28
☐	1509	Kari - Holland 45	☐	1002	Patti with Goose 11
☐	1111	Katherine 95	☐	D009	Patti with Goose 3
☐	1060	Kathy and Donnie 75	☐	1223	Pearl 84
☐	1025	Katie 19	☐	1395	Peony - August 70
☐	1036	Katlyn 36	☐	D007	Pink Missy 3
☐	1528	Keiki - Lani 51	☐	1107	Piper 28
☐	1026	Kerri 19	☐	1095	PM Collector Doll 6
☐	1112	Kiesha 96	☐	1200	Princess Melody 57

129

Alphabetical Listing by Subject

☐	1020	Princess Sincere 17				
☐	1518	Pualani 49			***Grandma***	
☐	1464	Pumpkin - October 64	☐	1085	Grandma Martha 26	
☐	1434	Pumpkin - October 67				
☐	1397	Pumpkin - October 71			***Grandpa***	
☐	1029	Rachel 91	☐	1118	Grandpa Bill 29	
☐	1626	Raspberry 40				
☐	1052	Rebecca 95			***Groom***	
☐	1611	Red and Blue Plaid 81	☐	1422	Blond Groom 29	
☐	1419	Red Riding Hood 80	☐	1493	Groom 31	
☐	1550	Regina 32	☐	1011	Jonny - 16" 14	
☐	1081	Robin 37	☐	1011	Jonny - 17" 14	
☐	1460	Rose - June 62	☐	1011	Jonny - 17" 14	
☐	1430	Rose - June 66	☐	1604	Jonny - 26" 34	
☐	1393	Rose - June 70				
☐	1090	Rosemary 92			***Hispanic***	
☐	1613	Royal Blue Plaid Rag Doll 82	☐	1023	Bethany - Hispanic 18	
☐	1225	Ruby 85	☐	1067	Brown Baby Hispanic 24	
☐	1632	Sadie - Softball 103	☐	1109	Hispanic Baby 28	
☐	1031	Sandy - Blue 20				
☐	1032	Sandy - White 20			***Mother***	
☐	1227	Sapphire 86	☐	1088	Carissa and Baby Tess 76	
☐	1445	Sara and Kara 37	☐	1057	Dawn and Rag Doll 23	
☐	1074	Sarah 25	☐	1030	Janet and Baby Sarah 74	
☐	1487	Seminole 78	☐	1044	Jessi and Baby Lisa 74	
☐	1959	September's Child 41	☐	1060	Kathy and Donnie 75	
☐	1503	Shannon - Ireland 43	☐	1082	Lori and Ginnie 75	
☐	1505	Shonnie - American Indian 43	☐	1048	Milly and Her New Baby Doll 22	
☐	1402	Shoshoni 79	☐	1101	Susan with Twins 75	
☐	1486	Sioux 77				
☐	1516	Sophie - Poland 48			***Nativity***	
☐	2012	Spiegel Exclusive 103	☐	1055	Daniel 5	
☐	1220	Star 53	☐	1555	Nativity Set 80	
☐	1211	Stephanie 52				
☐	1625	Strawberry 40			***Ornaments and Decorations***	
☐	1510	Sulu - Alaska 46	☐	2004	Carrie 54	
☐	1510a	Sulu - Alaska 46	☐	2003	Christie 54	
☐	1463	Sunny - September 64	☐	2009	Gold - Angel 55	
☐	1433	Sunny - September 67	☐	2010	Silver - Angel 56	
☐	1396	Sunny - September 70				
☐	1605	Sunshine 38			***Sports***	
☐	1101	Susan with Twins 75	☐	1631	Benson - Basketball 103	
☐	1635	Sydney - Soccer 103	☐	1634	Cassie - Cheerleader 103	
☐	D006	Taffy 2	☐	1633	Flint - Football 103	
☐	1513	Taya - India 47	☐	1630	Gordon - Golf 103	
☐	1414	Teacher 41	☐	1636	Hanford - Hockey 103	
☐	1014	Tiffany 16	☐	1499	Karate Boy 97	
☐	1629	Tina - Tennis 103	☐	1498	Karate Girl 97	
☐	1472	Tonya 97	☐	1632	Sadie - Softball 103	
☐	1047	Tracey 22	☐	1635	Sydney - Soccer 103	
☐	1607	Valerie 39	☐	1629	Tina - Tennis 103	
☐	1115	Victoria 81	☐	1498	Young Hee 31	
☐	1062	Viola 23	☐	1499	Young Ho 31	
☐	1456	Violet - February 61				
☐	1426	Violet - February 65			***Tree Toppers***	
☐	1072	Whitney - Winter 60	☐	2011	Angelica 56	
☐	1468	Winnie 30	☐	2002	Carrie 54	
☐	1484	Yakima 77	☐	2015	Celeste 56	
☐	1526	Yoim - Korea 50	☐	2001	Christy 53	
☐	1498	Young Hee 31	☐	2006	Harmony 55	
☐	1482	Zuni and Olla 76	☐	2008	Joy 55	
			☐	2007	Peace 55	
			☐	2005	Timmy 54	
		Graduation				
☐	1554	Graduate 32				
☐	1031	Sandy 20				
☐	1032	Sandy 20				

Notes

Notes

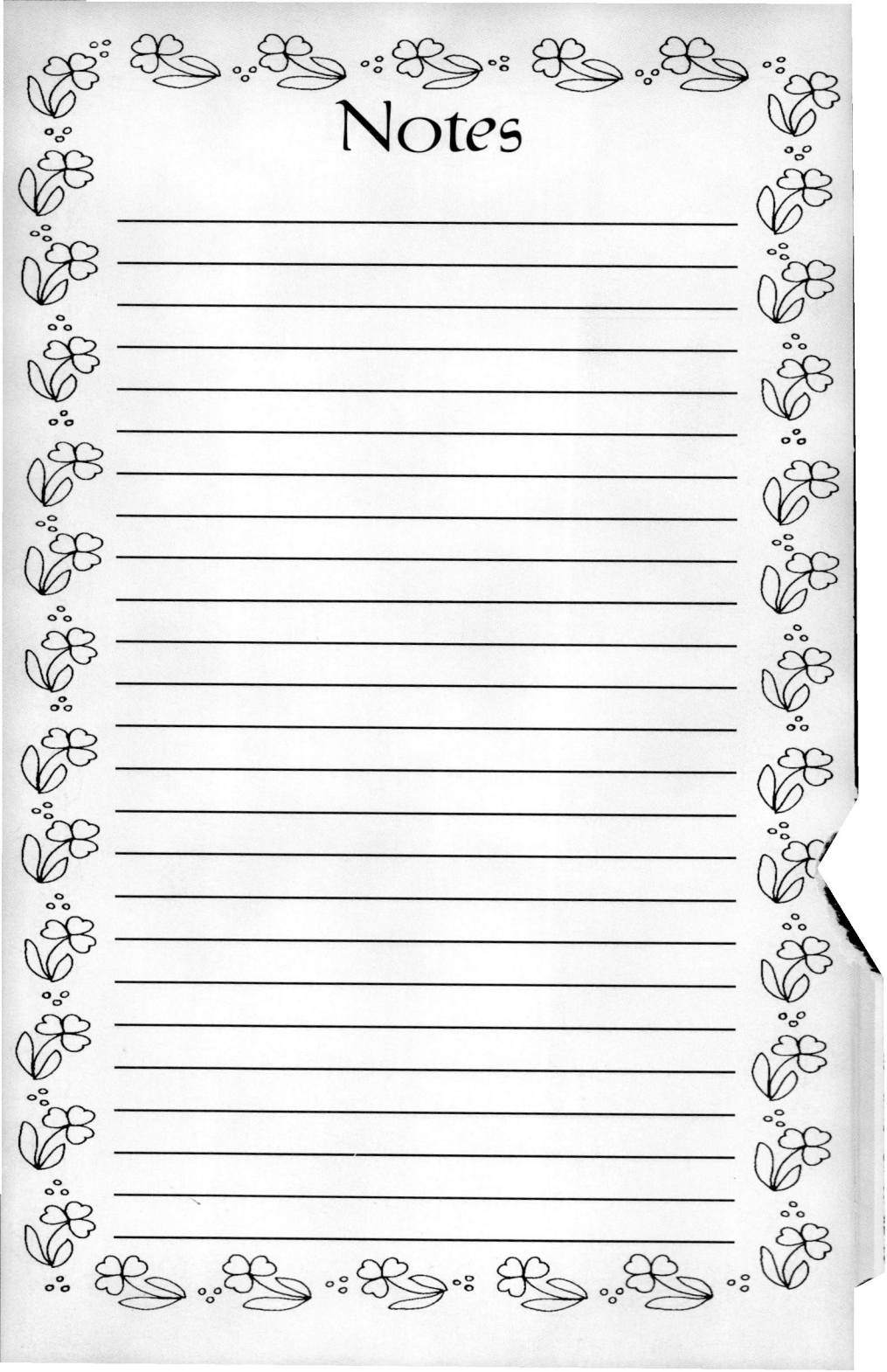

Notes

Save $5.00

$5.00 off the Weekly Collectors' Gazette™ when you send in this coupon for a 12 week subscription for $24.00.

OR

$5.00 off the Collectors' Bulletin™ magazine that now contains Precious Collectibles® (latest Precious Moments® news), when you send in this coupon with a 1 year subscription for $23.95.

When ordering the Weekly Collectors' Gazette™ or the Collectors' Bulletin™, you must include this coupon.
No phone orders. Redeemable by mail only. Coupon may not be duplicated.

Name: _____
Address: _____
City: _____ State: _____ Zip Code: _____
Phone: _____

☐ Check:
☐ Master/Visa/Discover #: _____
Expires: _____

No phone calls, please.
Send coupon with payment to:

Rosie Wells Enterprises, Inc.

22341 E. Wells Rd., Dept. J., Canton, IL 61520

©1997 Precious Moments, Inc. Licensee ENESCO CORP.